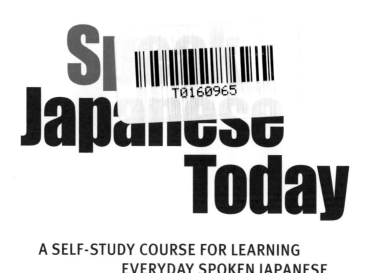

Speak Japanese Today

A SELF-STUDY COURSE FOR LEARNING
EVERYDAY SPOKEN JAPANESE

Taeko Kamiya

TUTTLE Publishing

Tokyo | Rutland, Vermont | Singapore

ABOUT TUTTLE
"Books to Span the East and West"

Our core mission at Tuttle Publishing is to create books which bring people together one page at a time. Tuttle was founded in 1832 in the small New England town of Rutland, Vermont (USA). Our fundamental values remain as strong today as they were then—to publish best-in-class books informing the English-speaking world about the countries and peoples of Asia. The world has become a smaller place today and Asia's economic, cultural and political influence has expanded, yet the need for meaningful dialogue and information about this diverse region has never been greater. Since 1948, Tuttle has been a leader in publishing books on the cultures, arts, cuisines, languages and literatures of Asia. Our authors and photographers have won numerous awards and Tuttle has published thousands of books on subjects ranging from martial arts to paper crafts. We welcome you to explore the wealth of information available on Asia at **www.tuttlepublishing.com**.

Published by Tuttle Publishing, an imprint of Periplus Editions (HK) Ltd.

www.tuttlepublishing.com

Copyright © 2010 by Periplus Editions (HK) Ltd.
Cover photo © 2008 John Cowie, Istockphoto

LCC Card No.: 2010927330
ISBN 978-4-8053-1115-8

22 21 20 19 18
10 9 8 7 6 5 4 3   1808MP
Printed in Singapore

TUTTLE PUBLISHING® is a registered trademark of Tuttle Publishing, a division of Periplus Editions (HK) Ltd.

Distributed by

North America, Latin America & Europe
Tuttle Publishing
364 Innovation Drive
North Clarendon, VT 05759-9436 U.S.A.
Tel: 1 (802) 773-8930
Fax: 1 (802) 773-6993
info@tuttlepublishing.com
www.tuttlepublishing.com

Japan
Tuttle Publishing
Yaekari Building, 3rd Floor
5-4-12 Osaki, Shinagawa-ku
Tokyo 141 0032
Tel: (81) 3 5437-0171
Fax: (81) 3 5437-0755
www.tuttle.co.jp

Asia Pacific
Berkeley Books Pte. Ltd.
61 Tai Seng Avenue #02-12
Singapore 534167
Tel: (65) 6280-1330
Fax: (65) 6280-6290
inquiries@periplus.com.sg
www.periplus.com

Contents

Acknowledgments

I am deeply indebted to the late Professor Roy Smith of Kobe University, Father Edward J. Kowrach and the Sisters of Holy Names for their help and guidance given to me many years ago. Their high standards and ideals not only have long been an inspiration to me, it also gave me the courage to undertake this project.

I am also grateful to the students of Japanese, present and past, at the Defense Language Institute. It has been their enthusiasm that has provided me with the stimulus to pursue better teaching methods over the years.

Last but not least, I wish to express my appreciation to Tuttle Publishing Company for making this publication possible.

Foreword

This book is intended for those who have little or no knowledge of Japanese. Whether you are traveling, working, or studying, you will discover it quite enjoyable and very rewarding to speak the language.

This book contains twenty lessons and two review chapters. Each new lesson presents a vocabulary list, a dialogue, additional vocabulary, and practice exercises. Note that lengthy grammatical explanations have been avoided—this is to enable the student to concentrate fully on the basic sentence patterns and useful everyday expressions that are introduced. Ample drills provide additional practice in this area.

Containing approximately 500 of the most commonly used words, this book covers the basics needed to get by in Japan. You will be able to exchange greetings, introduce yourself, board the right trains, order meals at restaurants, go shopping, talk about your holiday plans, and much more. Also, as you proceed through the lessons, you will be laying a firm foundation upon which further study of the language can be built.

Practice is the key to success. You will be surprised how much you can do with a basic vocabulary and a limited number of sentence patterns; all you have to do is to put them to work. Good luck and good wishes.

The Author

Pronunciation

VOWELS

The Japanese language has five vowels; **a**, **i**, **u**, **e**, and **o**. The vowels are pronounced as follows:

あ	**a**	as in f*a*ther
い	**i**	as in *e*at
う	**u**	as in r*u*le
え	**e**	as in m*e*t
お	**o**	as in s*o*lo

Long vowels—those whose sounds are sustained twice as long as regular vowels—are marked **ā**, **ii** or **ī**, **ū**, **ē**, and **ō**. Because it is easier to read, in this book the double **ii** is used instead of putting a macron over a single **i**.

CONSONANTS

Japanese consonants are pronounced about the same as English consonants. One exception is the Japanese **r**, which is pronounced like a combination of the English *r* and *l*, with the result being that it is similar to a **d** sound.

Double consonants as in 日光 **Nikko** (*famous tourist spot*) and 切手 **kitte** (*stamp*) are pronounced like the *k* sound in "boo*kk*eeper" and the *t* sound in "ho*t t*ub."

SYLLABLES

Each syllable should be pronounced clearly, although in ordinary speech, the **i** and **u** are often weakened as in 弾く **hiku** (*play*) and です **desu** (*am; is; are*).

When the consonant **n** is followed by a vowel or a **y** within a word, the **n** is pronounced like an independent syllable. Examples of this are 禁煙 **kin'en** (*nonsmoking*) and 本屋 **hon'ya** (*bookstore*). The mark (') is used to show a break between two syllables. In many cases, however, **hon'ya** is written as **hon-ya** because **-ya** is a suffix, meaning "a store."

JAPANESE SOUNDS

Following is a table of Japanese sounds. With the exception of the **n** sound, each sound is made up of a single vowel, a consonant followed by a vowel, or a consonant followed by a **y** or an **h**, and then a vowel.

Each sound is distinctly pronounced—thus *ai* (*love*) is pronounced in two syllables, **a-i**; 花 **hana** (*flower*) as **ha-na;** and 百 **hyaku** (*one hundred*) as **hya-ku**.

Study the following table and clearly pronounce each syllable aloud. Then proceed to the next page for more practice.

a あ	**i** い	**u** う	**e** え	**o** お
ka か	**ki** き	**ku** く	**ke** け	**ko** こ
ga が	**gi** ぎ	**gu** ぐ	**ge** げ	**go** ご
sa さ	**shi** し	**su** す	**se** せ	**so** そ
za ざ	**ji** じ	**zu** ず	**ze** ぜ	**zo** ぞ
ta た	**chi** ち	**tsu** つ	**te** て	**to** と
da だ	—	—	**de** で	**do** ど
na な	**ni** に	**nu** ぬ	**ne** ね	**no** の
ha は	**hi** ひ	**fu** ふ	**he** へ	**ho** ほ
ba ば	**bi** び	**bu** ぶ	**be** べ	**bo** ぼ
pa ぱ	**pi** ぴ	**pu** ぷ	**pe** ぺ	**po** ぽ
ma ま	**mi** み	**mu** む	**me** め	**mo** も
ya や	—	**yu** ゆ	—	**yo** よ
ra ら	**ri** り	**ru** る	**re** れ	**ro** ろ
wa わ	—	—	—	—
n ん	—	—	—	—
kya きゃ	—	**kyu** きゅ	—	**kyo** きょ
gya ぎゃ	—	**gyu** ぎゅ	—	**gyo** ぎょ
sha しゃ	—	**shu** しゅ	—	**sho** しょ
ja じゃ	—	**ju** じゅ	—	**jo** じょ
cha ちゃ	—	**chu** ちゅ	—	**cho** ちょ
nya にゃ	—	**nyu** にゅ	—	**nyo** にょ
hya ひゃ	—	**hyu** ひゅ	—	**hyo** ひょ
bya びゃ	—	**byu** びゅ	—	**byo** びょ
pya ぴゃ	—	**pyu** ぴゅ	—	**pyo** ぴょ
mya みゃ	—	**my** みゅ	—	**myo** みょ
rya りゃ	—	**ryu** りゅ	—	**ryo** りょ

EXERCISES

Practice pronouncing the following words.

Japanese cities:

東京	**Tō-kyo**	*Tokyo*
大阪	**Ō-sa-ka**	*Osaka*
京都	**Kyō-to**	*Kyoto*
広島	**Hi-ro-shi-ma**	*Hiroshima*

Japanese cooking:

寿司	**su-shi**	*vinegared rice and fish*
天ぷら	**te-n-pu-ra**	*deep-fried food*
刺身	**sa-shi-mi**	*sliced raw fish*

Japanese sports:

相撲	**su-mō**	*sumo*
柔道	**ju-dō**	*judo*
剣道	**ke-n-dō**	*Japanese fencing*

Loanwords:

アメリカ	**A-me-ri-ka**	*America*
カメラ	**ka-me-ra**	*camera*
ニュース	**nyū-su**	*news*
ゴルフ	**go-ru-fu**	*golf*
ビール	**bii-ru**	*beer*
コーヒー	**kō-hii**	*coffee*
チップ	**chi-p-pu***	*tip (gratuity)*
サッカー	**sa-k-kā***	*soccer*

* These are examples of double consonants.

A NOTE ON THE PUNCTUATION USED IN THIS BOOK

Below is an explanation of how this book uses semi-colons and slashes in word definitions.

Semi-colon: to separate short entries

です **desu** *is; am; are*   元気 **genki** *healthy; fine*

Slashes: to separate interchangeable words within a phrase

戸田さん **Toda-san** *Mr./Mrs./Miss Toda (Mr. Toda, Mrs. Toda, Miss Toda)*

いただます **Itadakimasu** *I will receive/have. (I will receive. I will have.)*

to separate long entries

お元気ですか **O-genki desu ka?** *How are you?/Are you well?*

How Do You Do?

VOWELS

Study these words and clearly pronounce them aloud. Then proceed to the dialogue.

こんばんは	**Konbanwa.**	*Good evening.*
はじめまして	**Hajimemashite.**	*How do you do?* (used when meeting someone for the first time)
どうぞよろしく	**Dōzo yoroshiku.**	*Glad to meet you.* (*lit.,* Please give favors to me.)
どうぞ	**dōzo**	*please* (used when asking something or when offering something)
あの	**ano**	*that*
ひと	**hito**	*person*
あのひと	**ano hito**	*that person* (he or she)
だれ	**dare**	*who*
こちら	**kochira**	*this person/thing*
佐藤	**Satō**	(a family name)
戸田さん	**Toda-san**	*Mr./Mrs./Miss Toda*
さん	**-san**	(an honorific suffix added to another person's given name, family name, or full name)
カーターさん	**Kātā-san**	*Mr./Mrs./Miss Carter*
アメリカ	**Amerika**	*America*
朝日新聞	**Asahi Shinbun**	*Asahi Newspaper* (one of the leading Japanese newspapers)
記者	**kisha**	*reporter*
は	**wa**[1]	(a topic marker)
です	**desu**	*is; am; are*
か	**ka?**[2]	(a question marker)
の	**no**[3]	*of; for*

POINTS TO REMEMBER

1. NOUN + **wa**: as for NOUN
   Wa is a particle attached to the topic (or subject) of a sentence. The topic can be anything—a person, a thing, the weather—that comes at the beginning of the sentence. This topic is followed by **wa**.

   EXAMPLE: あの人は記者です。
   Ano hito wa kisha desu.
   That person is a reporter.

2. **Ka** is a question marker. **Ka** at the end of a sentence turns it into a question.

   EXAMPLE: あの記者は誰ですか。
   Ano kisha wa dare desu ka?
   Who is that reporter?

3. NOUN (A) + **no** + NOUN (B): NOUN (B) of NOUN (A)
   [NOUN (A) + **no**] modifies NOUN (B).

   EXAMPLE: 朝日新聞の記者
   Asahi Shinbun no kisha
   a reporter for the Asahi Newspaper

4. In general, Japanese nouns do not have plural forms and there are no articles. Therefore, English words such as "a," "the," "some," and "any," are not translated.

5. The subject is often omitted in Japanese.

DIALOGUE
Study the dialogue below. Practice until you no longer need to refer to the Japanese half.

Carter : こんばんは。あの人は誰ですか。
   Konbanwa. Ano hito wa[1] dare desu ka[2]?
   Good evening. Who is that person? (*lit.,* As for that person, who is she?)

Satō : 戸田さんです。あの人は朝日新聞の記者です。
   Toda-san desu. Ano hito wa Asahi Shinbun no[3] kisha desu.
   It's Miss Toda. She is a[4] reporter for the Asahi Newspaper.

* * * * * *

Satō : 戸田さん、こちらはアメリカのカーターさんです。
Toda-san, kochira wa Amerika no Kātā-san desu.
Miss Toda, this is Mr. Carter of America.
カーターさん、こちらは朝日新聞社の戸田さんです。
Kātā-san, kochira wa Asahi Shinbun no Toda-san desu.
Mr. Carter, this is Miss Toda of the Asahi Newspaper.

Toda : はじめまして。戸田です。
Hajimemashite. Toda desu.
How do you do? I[5] am Toda.
どうぞよろしく。
Dōzo yoroshīku.
Glad to meet you.

Carter : はじめまして。カーターです。
Hajimemashite. Kātā desu.
How do you do? I am Carter.
どうぞよろしく。
Dōzo yoroshiku.
Pleased to meet you.

ADDITIONAL WORDS

Study these new words and clearly pronounce them aloud. Then proceed to the exercises.

医者	**isha**	*doctor*
看護師	**kangoshi**	*nurse*
会社員	**kaisha-in**	*company employee*
作家	**sakka**	*writer*
先生	**sensei**	*teacher*
おはようございます。	**Ohayō gozaimasu.**	*Good morning.*
こんにちは。	**Konnichiwa.**	*Good day/afternoon.*
おやすみなさい。	**O-yasumi-nasai.**	*Good night.*
さようなら／さよなら。	**Sayōnara/Sayonara.**	*Goodbye.*
お元気ですか。	**O-genki desu ka?**	*How are you?/ Are you well?*
はい、元気です。	**Hai, genki desu.**	*Yes. I'm fine.*
お	**o-**	*(an honorific prefix used when referring to others)*
元気	**genki**	*healthy; fine*

失礼します/しました。	**Shitsurei shimasu/ shimashita.**[1]	*Excuse me for being/ having been impolite.*
失礼	**shitsurei**	*being impolite*
いただきます。	**Itadakimasu.**[2]	*I will receive/have.*
ごちそうさまでした。	**Gochisō-sama deshita.**[3]	*It was delicious.*

---

[1] **Shitsurei shimasu** 失礼します is said when leaving the table while others are still eating, when entering other people's rooms, or when walking in front of others. **Shitsurei shimashita** 失礼しました is said when returning to the room you left in the middle of a meeting or meal, or after bumping into someone.

[2] An expression of gratitude, **Itadakimasu** いただきます is said when receiving a gift or the like, or before eating or drinking.

[3] **Gochisō-sama deshita** ごちそうさまでした, also an expression of gratitude, is said after having finished eating or drinking.

EXERCISES

A. Practice saying the following sentences in Japanese. Repeat the exercises until you no longer need to refer to the Japanese half.

1. *Who is that person?*   **Ano hito wa dare desu ka?**   あの人は誰ですか。

   That is Miss Toda.   **Toda-san desu.**   戸田さんです。

   She is a reporter.   **Kisha desu.**   記者です。

   She is a nurse.   **Kangoshi desu.**   看護師です。

   She is a teacher.   **Sensei desu.**   先生です。

   She is a company employee.   **Kaisha-in desu.**   会社員です。

   She is a writer.   **Sakka desu.**   作家です。

   She is a doctor.   **Isha desu.**   医者です。

2. *This is Mr. Sato of the Asahi Newspaper.*   **Kochira wa Asahi Shinbun no Satō-san desu.**   こちらは朝日新聞 の佐藤さんです。

   This is Miss Toda of Tokyo.   **Kochira wa Tōkyō no Toda-san desu.**   こちらは東京の 戸田さんです。

   This is Mrs. Carter of America.   **Kochira wa Amerika no Kātā-san desu.**   こちらはアメリカの カーターさんです。

3. *Good morning.*   **Ohayō gozaimasu.**   おはようございます。

   Good afternoon.   **Konnichiwa.**   こんにちは。

Good evening.	**Konbanwa.**	こんばんは。
Good night.	**O-yasumi-nasai.**	おやすみなさい。
Goodbye.	**Sayōnara/Sayonara.**	さようなら／さよなら。
How are you?/	**O-genki desu ka?**	お元気ですか。
Are you well?		
Yes. I'm fine.	**Hai, genki desu.**	はい、元気です。
How do you do?	**Hajimemashite.**	はじめまして。
Glad to meet you.	**Dōzo yoroshiku.**	どうぞよろしく。
Excuse me.	**Shitsurei shimasu/ shimashita.**	失礼します／しました。
I will receive/have.	**Itadakimasu.**	いただきます。
It was delicious.	**Gochisō-sama deshita.**	ごちそうさまでした。
Please.	**Dōzo.**	どうぞ。

B. What would you say under the following circumstances?
1. You meet someone in the morning.
2. You meet someone in the afternoon.
3. You meet someone in the evening.
4. You offer someone a cup of tea.
5. You are leaving the table for a moment.
6. You have enjoyed a delicious meal.
7. You introduce Mr. Carter to Miss Toda.
8. You are introduced to someone. (Your name is Carter.)
9. You are going to retire for the night.
10. You bump into someone in the hallway.

ANSWERS

B.
1. **Ohayō gozaimasu.** おはようございます。
2. **Konnichiwa.** こんにちは。
3. **Konbanwa.** こんばんは。
4. **Dōzo.** どうぞ。
5. **Shitsurei shimasu.** 失礼します。
6. **Gochisō-sama deshita.** ごちそうさまでした。
7. **Toda-san, kochira wa Kātā-san desu.** 戸田さん、こちらはカーターさんです。
8. **Hajimemashite. Kātā desu. Dōzo yoroshiku.** はじめまして。カーターです。どうぞよろしく。
9. **O-yasumi-nasai.** おやすみなさい。
10. **Shitsurei shimashita.** 失礼しました。

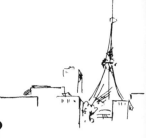

LESSON 2

What Is That?

VOCABULARY

Study these words and clearly pronounce them aloud. Then proceed to the dialogue.

どこ	**doko**	*where*
まで	**made**[1]	*to*
あれ	**are***	*that (one)**
何	**nan(i)**[2]	*what*
東京駅	**Tōkyō Eki**	*Tokyo Station*
東京	**Tōkyō**	(capital of Japan)
駅	**eki**	*station*
歌舞伎座	**Kabuki-za**	*the Kabuki Theater*
歌舞伎	**kabuki**	*traditional Japanese drama*
建物	**tatemono**	*building*
あなた	**anata**	*you*
私	**watashi**	*I*
アメリカ人	**Amerika-jin**	*American* (person)
人	**-jin**	(a suffix used for nationality)
方	**kata**	*person* (polite)
アメリカの方	**Amerika no kata**	*person of America* (a polite phrase for アメリカ人 **Amerika-jin**)

* The pronoun **are** becomes **ano** when it modifies a following noun (*see* Lesson 1, Vocabulary).

DIALOGUE

Study the dialogue below. Practice until you no longer need to refer to the Japanese half.

Cab driver　:　どこまで(ですか)。
　　　　　　　Doko made[1] **(desu ka)?**
　　　　　　　Where (are you going) to?

Tourist   : 東京駅まで(です)。
Tōkyō Eki made (desu).
To Tokyo Station.
Cab driver : 貴方はアメリカの方ですか。
Anata wa Amerika no kata desu ka?
Are you an American? (lit., a person of America*)*
Tourist   : はい、私はアメリカ人です。
Hai, watashi wa Amerika-jin desu.
Yes, I am an American.

* * * * * *

Tourist   : あれは何ですか。
Are wa nan² desu ka?
What is that?
Cab driver : あの建物(ですか)。
Ano tatemono (desu ka)?
That building?
あれは歌舞伎座です。
Are wa Kabuki-za desu.
That is the Kabuki Theater.

 POINTS TO REMEMBER

1. NOUN + **made**: to/till NOUN
   Made is used to indicate an ending point in time and place.
   EXAMPLE: 東京駅までです。
        Tōkyō Eki made desu.
        To Tokyo Station.
   For more examples, *see* Lesson 5.

2. Before **d**, **t**, and **n**, **nani** (what) becomes **nan**.
   EXAMPLES: あれは何ですか。
        Are wa nan desu ka?
        What is this?
        何の本ですか。
        Nan no hon desu ka?
        What is this book about? (lit., This book is what?)

ADDITIONAL WORDS

Study these new words and clearly pronounce them aloud. Then proceed to the exercises.

ドイツ	**Doitsu**	*Germany*
ドイツ人	**Doitsu-jin**	*German* (person)
フランス	**Furansu**	*France*
フランス人	**Furansu-jin**	*French* (person)
イギリス	**Igirisu**	*England*
イギリス人	**Igirisu-jin**	*English* (person)
日本	**Nippon/Nihon**	*Japan*
日本人	**Nippon-jin/Nihon-jin**	*Japanese* (person)
銀行	**ginkō**	*bank*
空港	**kūkō**	*airport*
大使館	**taishi-kan**	*embassy*
帝国ホテル	**Teikoku Hoteru**	*the Imperial Hotel*
ホテル	**hoteru**	*hotel*
これ	**kore***	*this (one)*
この	**kono**	*this*
いいえ	**iie**	*no*

* Just as **are** becomes **ano**, the pronoun **kore** becomes **kono** when it modifies a following noun.

EXAMPLE: このホテル **kono hoteru** (*this hotel*)

EXERCISES

A. Practice saying the following sentences in Japanese. Repeat the exercises until you no longer need to refer to the Japanese half.

1. *Where (are you going) to?*	**Doko made (desu ka)?**	どこまで(ですか)。
To the Imperial Hotel.	**Teikoku Hoteru made (desu).**	帝国ホテルまで (です)。
To Tokyo Station.	**Tōkyō Eki made.**	東京駅まで。
To the airport.	**Kūkō made.**	空港まで。
2. *Are you an American?*	**Anata wa Amerika no kata desu ka?**	あなたはアメリカの方ですか。
Are you a Japanese?	**Anata wa Nihon no kata desu ka?**	あなたは日本の方ですか。
Are you French?	**Anata wa Furansu no kata desu ka?**	あなたはフランスの方ですか。
3. *Yes, I am an American.*	**Hai, watashi wa Amerika-jin desu.**	はい、私はアメリカ人です。
Yes, I am English.	**Hai, watashi wa Igirisu-jin desu.**	はい、私はイギリス人です。
Yes, I am German.	**Hai, watashi wa Doitsu-jin desu.**	はい、私はドイツ人です。
4. *Are you English?*	**Anata wa Igirisu no kata desu ka?**	あなたはイギリス人ですか。
No. I am French.	**Iie. Watashi wa Furansu-jin desu.**	いいえ、私はフランス人です。
No. 1 am German.	**Iie. Watashi wa Doitsu-jin desu.**	いいえ、私はドイツ人です。
5. *What is that building?*	**Ano taemono wa nan desu ka?**	あの建物はなんですか。
That is the Kabuki Theater.	**Are wa Kabuki-za desu.**	あれは歌舞伎座です。
That is a bank.	**Are wa ginkō desu.**	あれは銀行です。

6. *What is this building?* **Kono tatemono wa nan desu ka?** この建物はなんですか。

This is the Imperial Hotel. **Kore wa Teikoku Hoteru desu.** これは帝国ホテルです。

This is the embassy. **Kore wa taishi-kan desu.** これは大使館です。

B. Answer the following questions using the cue words.

1. **Doko made desu ka?**
   どこまでですか。
   (airport) _____

2. **Anata wa Doitsu no kata desu ka?**
   あなたはドイツの方ですか。
   Hai, _____

3. **Anata wa Furansu no kata desu ka?**
   あなたはフランスの方ですか。
   (American) **Iie.** _____

   (English) **Iie.** _____

4. **Ano tatemono wa nan desu ka?**
   あの建物はなんですか。
   (embassy) **Are wa** _____

5. **Kono tatemono wa nan desu ka?**
   この建物はなんですか。
   (Kabuki Theater) **Kore wa** _____

ANSWERS

B.
1. **Kūkō made desu.** 空港までです。
2. **Hai, watashi wa Doitsu-jin desu.** はい、私はドイツ人です。
3. **Iie. Watashi wa Amerika-jin desu.** いいえ、私はアメリカ人です。
   Iie. Watashi wa Igirisu-jin desu. いいえ、私はイギリス人です。
4. **Are wa taishi-kan desu.** あれは大使館です。
5. **Kore wa Kabuki-za desu.** これは歌舞伎座です。

LESSON 3

Where Is the Bank?

VOCABULARY

Study these words and clearly pronounce them aloud. Then proceed to the dialogue.

すみません。	**Sumimasen.**	*Excuse me.* (used to get someone's attention)
ああ	**ā**	*oh*
そうです	**sō desu**	*it's so; that's right*
ああ、そうですか。	**Ā, sō desu ka?**	*Oh, I see/Is that so?*
ありがとう。	**Arigatō.**	*Thank you.*
どういたしまして。	**Dō-itashimashite.**	*You are welcome.*
あそこ	**asoko**	*over there*
郵便局	**yūbin-kyoku**	*post office*
本屋	**hon-ya**	*bookstore*
本	**hon**	*book*
屋	**-ya**	*(a suffix used for stores)*
前	**mae**	*front*
~の前	**~ no mae**	*in front of ~*
右	**migi**	*right*
~の右	**~ no migi**	*on/to the right of ~*

DIALOGUE

Study the dialogue below. Practice until you no longer need to refer to the Japanese half.

Tourist : すみません。銀行はどこですか。
Sumimasen. Ginkō wa doko desu ka?
Excuse me. Where is the bank?

Passerby : あそこです。郵便局の前です。
Asoko desu. Yūbin-kyoku no mae desu.
It's[1] in front of the post office.

Tourist : 本屋は。
Hon-ya wa?
How about a bookstore?

Passerby : 銀行の右です。
Ginkō no migi desu.
It's to the right of the bank.

Tourist : ああ、そうですか。ありがとう。
Ā, sō desu ka? Arigatō.
Oh, I see. Thank you.

Passerby : どういたしまして。
Dō-itashimashite.
You are welcome.

 POINTS TO REMEMBER

1. As noted in Lesson 1, in Japanese the subject is often omitted.

ADDITIONAL WORDS

Study these new words and clearly pronounce them aloud. Then proceed to the exercises.

ここ	**koko**	*here*
左	**hidari**	*left*
〜の左	**~ no hidari**	*on/to the left of ~*
後ろ	**ushiro**	*back*
〜の後ろ	**~ no ushiro**	*at the back of/behind ~*
病院	**byōin**	*hospital*
映画館	**eiga-kan**	*movie theater*
学校	**gakkō**	*school*
花屋	**hana-ya**	*flower shop*
パン屋	**pan-ya**	*bakery*
タクシー乗り場	**takushii-noriba**	*taxi stand*
お手洗い	**o-tearai***	*restroom*
電話	**denwa**	*telephone*

* The honorific prefix **o-** is used primarily to refer to others (*see* Lesson 1). It also is used to form polite expressions for certain things in everyday life.
EXAMPLES: お花 **o-hana** (*flower*); お電話 **o-denwa** (*telephone*).

EXERCISES

A. Practice saying the following sentences in Japanese. Repeat the exercises until you no longer need to refer to the Japanese half.

1. *Where is the taxi stand?*   **Takushii-noriba wa doko desu ka?**   タクシー乗り場はどこですか。

   Where is the bank?   **Ginkō wa doko desu ka?**   銀行はどこですか。

   Where is the hospital?   **Byōin wa doko desu ka?**   病院はどこですか。

   Where is the telephone?   **Denwa wa doko desu ka?**   電話はどこですか。

   Where is the restroom?   **O-tearai wa doko desu ka?**   お手洗いはどこですか。

2. *It's here/over there.*   **Koko/Asoko desu.**   ここ／あそこです。

   It's to the left of the post office.   **Yūbin-kyoku no hidari desu.**   郵便局の左です。

   It's behind the post office.   **Yūbin-kyoku no ushiro desu.**   郵便局の後ろです。

   It's to the right of the post office.   **Yūbin-kyoku no migi desu.**   郵便局の右です。

   It's in front of the post office.   **Yūbin-kyoku no mae desu.**   郵便局の前です。

3. *It's in front of the school.*   **Gakkō no mae desu.**   学校の前です。

   It's to the right of the bakery.   **Pan-ya no migi desu.**   パン屋の右です。

   It's to the left of the movie theater.   **Eiga-kan no hidari desu.**   映画館の左です。

   It's behind the flower shop.   **Hana-ya no ushiro desu.**   花屋の後ろです。

4. *Excuse me.*   **Sumimasen.**   すみません。

   Thank you.   **Arigatō.**   ありがとう。

   You're welcome.   **Dō-itashimashite.**   どういたしまして。

   Oh, I see.   **Ā, sō desu ka?**   ああ、そうですか。

B. Fill in the blanks using the cue words.

1. **Sumimasen. Ginkō wa doko desu ka?**
   すみません。銀行はどこですか。
   (behind that building) **Ano** _____ **no** _____ **desu.**

2. **Sumimasen. O-tearai wa doko desu ka?**
   すみません。お手洗いはどこですか。
   (over there) _____ **desu.**

3. **Takushii-noriba wa doko desu ka?**
   タクシー乗り場はどこですか。
   (in front of the station) _____ **no** _____ **desu.**

4. **Eiga-kan wa doko desu ka?**
   映画館はどこですか。
   (behind the post office) _____

5. **Denwa wa doko desu ka?**
   電話はどこですか。
   (to the left of the bakery) _____

6. **Hon-ya wa doko desu ka?**
   本屋はどこですか。
   (to the right of the flower shop) _____

7. **Ā, sō desu ka?**
   ああ、そうですか。
   (Thank you.) _____

8. (You are welcome.) _____

ANSWERS

B.
1. **tatemono, ushiro** 建物、後ろ 。
2. **Asoko** あそこ
3. **Eki, mae** 駅、前
4. **Yūbin-kyoku no ushiro desu.** 郵便局の後ろです。
5. **Pan-ya no hidari desu.** パン屋の左です。
6. **Hana-ya no migi desu.** 花屋の右です。
7. **Arigatō.** ありがとう。
8. **Dō-itashimashite.** どういたしまして。

What Time Is the Next Hikari?

VOCABULARY

Study these words and clearly pronounce them aloud. Then proceed to the dialogue.

新幹線	**Shinkansen**	*the Shinkansen* (the "bullet train")
ひかり	**Hikari**	(name of a super express *Shinkansen*)
博多行き	**Hakata-yuki**	(train) *for Hakata*
次	**tsugi**	*next*
電車	**densha**	*train*
次の電車	**tsugi no densha**	*next train*
～よ。	**～ yo.**[1]	(a particle used for emphasis meaning "I assure you.")
～ね。	**～ ne.**[2]	*～ isn't it?*
何時	**nan-ji**	*what time*
時	**-ji**	(a suffix used for o'clock/ hours)
九時	**ku-ji**[3]	*9 o'clock*
何番線	**nan-ban-sen**	*what track*
番	**-ban**	(a suffix used for ordinal numbers)
線	**-sen**	(a suffix used for tracks)
15番線	**jū-go-ban-sen**	*track no. 15*
どうもありがとう。	**Dōmo arigatō.**[4]	*Thank you.*

DIALOGUE

Study the dialogue below. Practice until you no longer need to refer to the Japanese half.

Tourist ： 新幹線はここですか。
Shinkansen wa koko desu ka?
Is this where you catch the Shinkansen? (*lit.*, Is the *Shinkansen* here?)

Man ： はい、ここですよ。
Hai, koko desu yo.[1]
Yes, it is. (I assure you.)

Tourist ： 博多行きは何時ですか。
Hakata-yuki wa nan-ji desu ka?
What time is the train for Hakata?

Man ： 「ひかり」ですね。次の電車は九時です。
Hikari desu ne.[2] **Tsugi no densha wa ku-ji**[3] **desu.**
Hikari, isn't it? The next train is at 9:00.

Tourist ： 何番線ですか。
Nan-ban-sen desu ka?
What track is it?

Man ： 15番線です。
Jū-go-ban-sen desu.
It's track no. 15.

Tourist ： どうもありがとう。
Dōmo arigatō.[4]
Thank you.

 POINTS TO REMEMBER

1. **Yo** is an end-of-a-sentence particle meaning "I assure you."
   Yo adds emphasis to the sentence.
   EXAMPLE: あそこですよ。
   Asoko desu yo.
   It's over there, I tell you.

2. **Ne** is an end-of-a-sentence particle meaning "isn't it" or "aren't you?"
   EXAMPLE: 次の電車ですね。
   Tsugi no densha desu ne.
   It's the next train, isn't it?

3. While the 24-hour timetable is used for trains, normally one would state time in the regular way.

> EXAMPLE: 今三時です。
> **Ima san-ji desu.**
> *It's 3:00 now.*

4. For "thank you," you can say ありがとう **arigatō**, どうも **dōmo**, or どうもありがとう **dōmo arigatō**. **Dōmo arigatō**, being the politest, is recommended for the student to use because it is appropriate for all situations.

ADDITIONAL WORDS

Numbers from 10 to 100 are formed by combining two numbers. To make 11, combine **jū** (10) and **ichi** (1); to make 20, combine **ni** (2) and **jū** (10).

Study these basic numbers and clearly pronounce them aloud. Then proceed to studying the time-related words.

Cardinal Numbers		
一	**ichi**	*1*
二	**ni**	*2*
三	**san**	*3*
四	**shi/yon**	*4*
五	**go**	*5*
六	**roku**	*6*
七	**shichi/nana**	*7*
八	**hachi**	*8*
九	**ku/kyū**	*9*
十	**jū**	*10*
十一	**jū-ichi**	*11*
十二	**jū-ni**	*12*
二十四	**ni-jū-shi/ni-jū-yon**	*24*
三十七	**san-jū-shichi/san-jū-nana**	*37*
四十九	**yon-jū-ku/yon-jū-kyū**	*49*

	O'clock (-ji)	
一時	**ichi-ji**	*1:00*
二時	**ni-ji**	*2:00*
三時	**san-ji**	*3:00*
四時	**yo-ji**	*4:00*
五時	**go-ji**	*5:00*
六時	**roku-ji**	*6:00*
七時	**shichi-ji/nana-ji**	*7:00*
八時	**hachi-ji**	*8:00*
九時	**ku-ji***	*9:00*
十時	**jū-ji**	*10:00*
十一時	**jū-ichi-ji**	*11:00*
十二時	**jū-ni-ji**	*12:00*
十三時	**jū-san-ji**	*13:00***
十四時	**jū-yo-ji**	*14:00*
十五時	**ju-go-ji**	*15:00*
十七時	**jū-shichi-ji/jū-nana-ji**	*17:00*
十九時	**jū-ku-ji**	*19:00*
午前	**gozen**	*A.M. (morning)*
午前六時	**gozen roku-ji**	*6 A.M.*
午後	**gogo**	*P.M. (afternoon)*
午後八時	**gogo hachi-ji**	*8 P.M.*
今	**ima**	*now*

*   This word appears in the dialogue.

** This is based on a 24-hour clock system, which runs from midnight. Hence 13:00 is equivalent to 1 P.M.

Minutes (-fun/pun)		
一分	**ip-pun**	*1 minute*
二分	**ni-fun**	*2 minutes*
三分	**san-pun**	*3 minutes*
四分	**yon-pun**	*4 minutes*
五分	**go-fun**	*5 minutes*
六分	**rop-pun**	*6 minutes*
七分	**shichi-fun/nana-fun**	*7 minutes*
八分	**hachi-fun/hap-pun**	*8 minutes*
九分	**kyū-fun**	*9 minutes*
十分	**jup-pun/jip-pun**	*10 minutes*
十五分	**jū-go-fun**	*15 minutes*
二十分	**ni-jup-pun/ni-jip-pun**	*20 minutes*
三十分	**san-jup-pun/san-jip-pun**	*30 minutes*
午前十時十五分	**gozen jū-ji jū-go-fun**	*10:15 A.M.*
午後九時三十分	**gogo ku-ji san-jup-pun**	*9:30 P.M.*
九時半	**ku-ji-han**	*9:30 P.M.*
半	**-han**	*half (past)*

EXERCISES

A. Practice saying the following exercises in Japanese. Repeat the exercises until you no longer need to refer to the Japanese half.

1. *What time is it now?*   **Ima nan-ji desu ka?**   今何時ですか。
   It's 3:00.   **San-ji desu.**   三時です。
   It's 7:00.   **Shichi-ji desu.**   七時です。
   It's 9:00.   **Ku-ji desu.**   九時です。

2. *What time is the*   **Hakata-yuki wa**   博多行きは
      train for Hakata?   **nan-ji desu ka?**   何時ですか。
   What time is the   **Tōkyō-yuki wa**   東京行きは
      train for Tokyo?   **nan-ji desu ka?**   何時ですか。

3. *What time is the*   **Tsugi no densha wa**   次の電車は
      next train?   **nan-ji desu ka?**   何時ですか。
   It's at 0800 hours.   **Hachi-ji desu.**   八時です。
   It's at 1200 hours.   **Jū-ni-ji desu.**   十二時です。
   It's at 1304 hours.   **Jū-san-ji yon-pun desu.**   十三時四分です。
   It's at 1630 hours.   **Jū-roku-ji san-jup-pun**   十六時三十分
      desu. (*or* **jū-roku-ji**   です。
      san-jip-pun)

4. *What track is the next Hikari?* | **Tsugi no Hikari wa nan-ban-sen desu ka?** | 次の「ひかり」は何番線ですか。
   It's track no. 15. | **Jū-go-ban-sen desu.** | 15線です。
   It's track no. 14. | **Jū-yon-ban-sen desu.** | 14線です。
   It's track no. 19. | **Jū-kyū-ban-sen desu.** | 19番線です。

5. *What time is school?* | **Gakkō wa nan-ji desu ka?** | 学校は何時ですか。
   It's at 8:30 A.M. | **Gozen hachi-ji-han desu.** | 午前八時半です。
   It's at 9:05 A.M. | **Gozen ku-ji go-fun desu.** | 午前九時五分です。
   It's at 10:20 A.M. | **Gozen jū-ji ni-jup-pun desu.** | 午前十時二十分です。

6. *What time is the movie?* | **Eiga wa nan-ji desu ka?** | 映画は何時ですか。
   It's at 1:10 P.M. | **Gogo ichi-ji jup-pun desu.** | 午後一時十分です。
   It's at 6:30 P.M. | **Gogo roku-ji-han desu.** | 午後六時半です。
   It's at 7:15 P.M. | **Gogo shichi-ji jū-go-fun desu.** | 午後七時十五分です。

B. Answer the following questions using the cue words.

1. **Ima nan-ji desu ka?** 今何時ですか。(8:00) _____
2. **Tsugi no densha wa nan-ji desu ka?** 次の電車は何時ですか。(11:30) _____
3. **Tsugi no Hikari wa nan-ban-sen desu ka?** 次の「ひかり」は何番線ですか。(track no. 17) _____
4. **Gakkō wa nan-ji desu ka?** 学校は何時ですか。(9:30 A.M.)
5. **Eiga wa nan-ji desu ka?** 映画は何時ですか。(7:15 P.M.)
6. **Ōsaka-yuki wa nan-ji desu ka?** 大阪行きは何時ですか。(16:40)

ANSWERS
B.
1. **Hachi-ji desu.** 八時です。
2. **Jū-ichi-ji san-jup-pun desu.** 十一時三十分です。(*or* **Jū-ichi-ji-han desu.**)
3. **Jū-nana-ban-sen desu.** 17番線です。
4. **Gozen ku-ji-han desu.** 午前九時半です。
5. **Gogo shichi-ji jū-go-fun desu.** 午後七時十五分です。
6. **Jū-roku-ji yon-jup-pun desu.** 十六時四十分です。

LESSON 5

How Many Hours Is It?

VOCABULARY

Study these words and clearly pronounce them aloud. Then proceed to the dialogue.

から	**kara**[1]	*from*
〜から〜まで	**~ kara ~ made**	*from ~ to/till ~*
何時間	**nan-jikan**	*how many hours*
時間	**-jikan**	(a suffix used for hours)
三時間	**san-jikan**	*3 hours*
四時間	**yo-jikan**	*4 hours*
で	**de**[2]	*by means of; in; with*
タクシーで	**takushii de**	*by taxi*
〜ぐらい	**~ gurai**[3]	*about ~* (approximate quantity)
十五分ぐらい	**jū-go-fun gurai**	*about 15 minutes*
近い	**chikai**	*near*
大阪	**Ōsaka**	*Osaka* (a city name)
大阪城	**Ōsaka-jō**	*Osaka Castle*
こだま	**Kodama**	(name of a limited express *Shinkansen*)

DIALOGUE

Study the dialogue below. Practice until you no longer need to refer to the Japanese half.

Jones : 東京から大阪まで何時間ですか。

Tōkyō kara[1] **Osaka made nan-jikan desu ka?**

From Tokyo to Osaka, how many hours is it?

Sato : 「ひかり」は三時間です。

Hikari wa san-jikan desu.

For the Hikari, it is 3 hours.

「こだま」は四時間です。

Kodama wa yo-jikan desu.

For the Kodama, it is 4 hours.

Jones : 大阪城は駅から近いですか。

Ōsaka-jō wa eki kara chikai desu ka?

Is the Osaka Castle near from the station?

Sato : はい、近いです。タクシーで十五分くらいです。

Hai, chikai desu. Takushii de² jū-go-fun gurai³ desu.

Yes, it's near. It is about 15 minutes by taxi.

 POINTS TO REMEMBER

1. NOUN + **kara**: from NOUN

   Kara is used to indicate a starting point in place and time.

   EXAMPLES: 東京から三時間です。

   > **Tōkyō kara san-jikan desu.**
   > *From Tokyo it's 3 hours.*
   > 会社は九時からです。
   > **Kaisha wa ku-ji kara desu.**
   > *The company is [open] from 9:00.*
   > 会議は午前八時から九時までです。
   > **Kaigi wa gozen hachi-ji kara ku-ji made desu.**
   > *The conference will be from 8:00 A.M. to 9:00.*

2. NOUN + **de**: by means of/in/with NOUN

   De is used to indicate an instrument or means.

   EXAMPLE: タクシーで十五分くらいです。

   > **Takushii de jū-go-fun gurai desu.**
   > *It's about 15 minutes by taxi.*

   De has another function which will be discussed in Lesson 13.

3. NUMBER + **gurai**

   Gurai is added to a number to indicate an approximate quantity.

   EXAMPLE: 十五分くらいです。

   > **Jū-go-fun gurai desu.**
   > *It's about 15 minutes.*

ADDITIONAL WORDS

Study these new words and clearly pronounce them aloud. Then proceed to the exercises.

バス	**basu**	*bus*
地下鉄	**chika-tetsu**	*subway*
船	**fune**	*ship*
飛行機	**hikō-ki**	*airplane*

デパート	**depāto**	*department store*
会社	**kaisha**	*company*
図書館	**tosho-kan**	*library*
会議	**kaigi**	*conference*
コンサート	**konsāto**	*concert*
何分	**nan-pun**	*how many minutes*
遠い	**tōi**	*far*

EXERCISES

A. Practice saying the following sentences in Japanese. Repeat the exercises until you no longer need to refer to the Japanese half.

1. *From Tokyo to Osaka, how many hours is it?* **Tōkyō kara Ōsaka made, nan-jikan desu ka?** 東京から大阪まで、何時間ですか。

2. *From the airport to the hotel, how many hours is it?* **Kūkō kara hoteru made, nan-jikan desu ka?** 空港からホテルまで、何時間ですか。

3. *From here to the post office, how many minutes is it?* **Koko kara yūbin-kyoku made, nan-pun desu ka?** ここから郵便局まで、何分ですか。

4. *From the bank to the department store, how many minutes is it?* **Ginkō kara depāto made, nan-pun desu ka?** 銀行からデパートまで、何分ですか。

5. *It's 10 minutes.* **Jup-pun desu.** 十分です。
   It's 45 minutes. **Yon-jū-go-fun desu.** 四十五分です。
   It's 3 hours. **San-jikan desu.** 三時間です。
   It's 1½ hours. **Ichi-jikan-han desu.** 一時間半です。

6. *Is it near/far from the library?* **Tosho-kan kara chikai/tōi desu ka?** 図書館から近い／遠いですか。
   Is it near/far from the company? **Kaisha kara chikai/tōi desu ka?** 会社から近い／遠いですか。
   Is it near/far from the school? **Gakkō kara chikai/tōi desu ka?** 学校から近い／遠いですか。

7. *It's 15 minutes by bus.* **Basu de jū-go-fun desu.** バスで十五分です。
   It's 30 minutes by subway. **Chika-tetsu de san-jup-pun desu.** 地下鉄で三十分です。
   It's about 2 hours by plane. **Hikō-ki de ni-jikan gurai desu.** 飛行機で二時間ぐらいです。
   It's about 4 hours by ship. **Fune de yo-jikan gurai desu.** 船で四時間ぐらいです。

8. *The concert is from 7 P.M. till 9:30.* **Konsāto wa gogo shichi-ji kara ku-ji-han made desu.** コンサートは午後七時から九時半までです。

9. *The conference is from 2:15 P.M. till 4:00.* **Kaigi wa gogo ni-ji jū-go-fun kara yo-ji made desu.** 会議は午後二時十五分から四時までです。

10. *The company is from 8 A.M. till 5 P.M.* **Kaisha wa gozen hachi-ji kara gogo go-ji made desu.** 会社は午前八時から午後五時までです。

B. Answer the following questions using the cue words.

1. **Tōkyō kara Ōsaka made, nan-jikan desu ka?**
   東京から大阪まで、何時間ですか。
   (3 hours, 4 hours) **Hikari wa** _____ .
   Kodama wa _____ .

2. **Kaisha wa eki kara chikai desu ka?**
   会社は駅から近いですか。
   Hai, _____ . **Iie,** _____ .

3. **Tosho-kan kara depāto made, nan-pun desu ka?**
   図書館からデパートまで、何分ですか。
   (about 15 minutes by subway) _____

4. **Hoteru kara kūkō made, nan-pun desu ka?**
   ホテルから空港まで、何分ですか。
   (about 30 minutes by bus) _____

5. **Kaigi wa nan-ji kara, nan-ji made desu ka?**
   会議は何時から、何時までですか。
   (9 A.M. till 1:30 P.M.) _____

ANSWERS

B.
1. **Hikari wa san-jikan desu.** 「ひかり」は三時間です。
   Kodama wa yo-jikan desu. 「こだま」は四時間です。
2. **Hai, chikai desu.** はい、近いです。
   Iie, tōi desu. いいえ、遠いです。
3. **Chika-tetsu de jū-go-fun gurai desu.** 地下鉄で十五分ぐらいです。
4. **Basu de san-jup-pun gurai desu.** バスで三十分ぐらいです。
5. **Gozen ku-ji kara gogo ichi-ji-han made desu.** 午前九時から午後一時半までです。

What Is the Date?

VOCABULARY

Study these words and clearly pronounce them aloud. Then proceed to the dialogue.

今日	**kyō**	*today*
何日	**nan-nichi**	*what day* (of the month)
日	**-nichi**	(a suffix used for days of the months)
三日	**mikka**	*the 3rd*
九日	**kokonoka**	*the 9th*
十八日	**jū-hachi-nichi**	*the 18th*
あなたの	**anata no**[1]	*your*
誕生日（誕生の日）	**tanjō-bi (tanjō no hi)**	*birthday (day of birth)*
日	**-bi**	(a suffix used for special days. When added to a noun, **hi** meaning "day," changes to **bi**.)
でした	**deshita**[2]	*was; were*
田中	**Tanaka**	(a family name)
山田さん	**Yamada-san**	*Mr./Mrs./Miss Yamada*

DIALOGUE

Study the dialogue below. Practice until you no longer need to refer to the Japanese half.

Smith : 今日は何日ですか。
　　　　Kyō wa nan-nichi desu ka?
　　　　What's the date today?

Tanaka : 九日です。
　　　　Kokonoka desu.
　　　　It's the 9th.

Smith : あなたの誕生日は何日ですか。
Anata no[1] tanjō-bi wa nan-nichi desu ka?
What's the date of your birthday?
Tanaka : 十八日です。
Jū-hachi-nichi desu.
It's the 18th.
Smith : 山田さんの誕生日は。
Yamada-san no tanjō-bi wa?
How about Mr. Yamada's birthday?
Tanaka : 三日でした。
Mikka deshita.[2]
It was the 3rd.

 POINTS TO REMEMBER

1. NOUN (A) + **no** + NOUN (B): NOUN (B) of NOUN (A)
   When NOUN (A) is a person, NOUN (A) + **no** indicates the possessive
   form—my, your, his, her, Mr. X's, etc. (*see* also Lesson 1)
   EXAMPLE: 今日は山田さんの誕生日です。
   Kyō wa Yamada-san no tanjō-bi desu.
   Today is Mr. Yamada's birthday.

2. A **wa** B **deshita**: A was B
   Deshita is the past tense of **desu.**
   EXAMPLE: きのうは十八日でした。
   Kinō wa jū-hachi-nichi deshita.
   Yesterday was the 18th.

ADDITIONAL WORDS

Study these time-related words and clearly pronounce them aloud. Then
proceed to the exercises.

一日	**tsuitachi** *the 1st*	九日	**kokonoka*** *the 9th*
二日	**futsuka** *the 2nd*	十日	**tōka** *the 10th*
三日	**mikka*** *the 3rd*	十一日	**jū-ichi-nichi** *the 11th*
四日	**yokka** *the 4th*	十二日	**jū-ni-nichi** *the 12th*
五日	**itsuka** *the 5th*	十三日	**jū-san-nichi** *the 13th*
六日	**muika** *the 6th*	十四日	**jū-yokka** *the 14th*
七日	**nanoka** *the 7th*	十五日	**jū-go-nichi** *the 15th*
八日	**yōka** *the 8th*	十六日	**jū-roku-nichi** *the 16th*

* These words appear in the dialogue.

十七日 **jū-shichi-nichi** *the 17th*
十八日 **jū-hachi-nichi*** *the 18th*
十九日 **jū-ku-nichi** *the 19th*
二十日 **hatsuka** *the 20th*
二十一日 **ni-jū-ichi-nichi** *the 21st*
二十二日 **ni-jū-ni-nichi** *the 22nd*
二十三日 **ni-jū-san-nichi** *the 23rd*
二十四日 **ni-jū-yokka** *the 24th*
二十五日 **ni-jū-go-nichi** *the 25th*
二十六日 **ni-jū-roku-nichi** *the 26th*
二十七日 **ni-jū-shichi-nichi** *the 27th*
二十八日 **ni-jū-hachi-nichi** *the 28th*
二十九日 **ni-jū-ku-nichi** *the 29th*
三十日 **san-jū-nichi** *the 30th*
三十一日 **san-jū-ichi-nichi** *the 31st*

きのう	**kinō**	*yesterday*
あした	**ashita**	*tomorrow*
結婚式	**kekkon-shiki**	*wedding ceremony*
式	**shiki**	*ceremony*
卒業式	**sotsugyō-shiki**	*graduation ceremony*

EXERCISES

A. Practice saying the following sentences in Japanese. Repeat the exercises until you no longer need to refer to the Japanese half.

1. *What day is today?* **Kyō wa nan-nichi desu ka?** 今日は何日ですか。

   What day is tomorrow? **Ashita wa nan-nichi desu ka?** あしたは何日ですか。

   What day is your birthday? **Anata no tanjō-bi wa nan-nichi desu ka?** あなたの誕生日は何日ですか。

   What day is Mr. Yamada's wedding? **Yamada-san no kekkon-shiki wa nan-nichi desu ka?** 山田さんの結婚式は何日ですか。

2. *What day was yesterday?* **Kinō wa nan-nichi deshita ka?** きのうは何日でしたか。

   What day was Miss Tanaka's birthday? **Tanaka-san no tanjō-bi wa nan-nichi deshita ka?** 田中さんの誕生日は何日でしたか。

What day was your graduation?	**Anata no sotsugyō-shiki wa nan-nichi deshita ka?**	あなたの卒業式は何日でしたか。
3. *Today is the 1st.*	**Kyō wa tsuitachi desu.**	今日は一日です。
Today is the 3rd.	**Kyō wa mikka desu.**	今日は三日です。
Today is the 7th.	**Kyō wa nanoka desu.**	今日は七日です。
4. *Tomorrow is the 2nd.*	**Ashita wa futsuka desu.**	あしたは二日です。
Tomorrow is the 4th.	**Ashita wa yokka desu.**	あしたは四日です。
Tomorrow is the 8th.	**Ashita wa yōka desu.**	あしたは八日です。
5. *Miss Yamada's birthday is the 5th.*	**Yamada-san no tanjō-bi wa itsuka desu.**	山田さんの誕生日は五日です。
My birthday is the 9th.	**Watashi no tanjōbi wa kokonoka desu.**	私の誕生日は九日です。
Mr. Tanaka's birthday is the 12th.	**Tanaka-san no tanjō-bi wa jū-ni-nichi desu.**	田中さんの誕生日は十二日です。
6. *Yesterday was the 18th.*	**Kinō wa jū-hachi-nichi deshita.**	きのうは十八日でした 。
Yesterday was the 20th.	**Kinō wa hatsuka deshita.**	きのうは二十日でした 。
Yesterday was the 24th.	**Kinō wa ni-jū-yokka deshita.**	きのうは二十四日でした。
7. *My graduation was the 6th.*	**Watashi no sotsugyō-shiki wa muika deshita.**	私の卒業式は六日でした。
Miss Tanaka's graduation was the 10th.	**Tanaka-san no sotsugyō-shiki wa tōka deshita.**	田中さんの卒業式は十日でした。
Mr. Yamada's graduation was the 30th.	**Yamada-san no sotsugyō-shiki wa san-jū-nichi deshita.**	山田さんの卒業式は三十日でした。

B. Answer the following questions using the cue words.

1. **Kyō wa nan-nichi desu ka?**
   今日は何日ですか。
   (5th) _____

2. **Ashita wa nan-nichi desu ka?**
   あしたは何日ですか。
   (6th) _____

3. **Kinō wa nan-nichi deshita ka?**
きのうは何日でしたか。
(4th) _____

4. **Anata no tanjō-bi wa nan-nichi desu ka?**
あなたの誕生日は何日ですか。
(13th) _____

5. **Yamada-san no sotsugyō-shiki wa nan-nichi deshita ka?**
山田さんの卒業式は何日でしたか。
(20th) _____

6. **Tanaka-san no kekkon-shiki wa nan-nichi deshita ka?**
田中さんの結婚式は何日でしたか。
(1st) _____

ANSWERS

B.
1. **(Kyō wa) itsuka desu.** (今日は) 五日です。
2. **(Ashita wa) muika desu.** (あしたは) 六日です。
3. **(Kinō wa) yokka deshita.** (きのうは) 四日でした。
4. **Jū-san-nichi desu.** 十三日です。
5. **Hatsuka deshita.** 二十日でした。
6. **Tsuitachi deshita.** 一日でした。

What Day of the Week Is Today?

VOCABULARY

Study these words and clearly pronounce them aloud. Then proceed to the dialogue.

何曜日	**nan-yōbi**	*what day of the week*
曜日	**-yōbi**	(a suffix used for the days of the week)
月曜日	**Getsu-yōbi**	*Monday*
火曜日	**Ka-yōbi**	*Tuesday*
水曜日	**Sui-yōbi**	*Wednesday*
木村	**Kimura**	(a family name)
送別会	**sōbetsu-kai**	*farewell party*
ではありません	**dewa arimasen**[1]	*is/am/are not*

DIALOGUE

Study the dialogue below. Practice until you no longer need to refer to the Japanese half.

Brown : 今日は何曜日ですか。
Kyō wa nan-yōbi desu ka?
What day of the week is it today?

Kimura : 月曜日です。
Getsu-yōbi desu.
It's Monday.

Brown : 山田さんの送別会は火曜日ですか。
Yamada-san no sōbetsu-kai wa Ka-yōbi desu ka?
Is Miss Yamada's party on Tuesday? (the farewell party for Miss Yamada)

Kimura : いいえ、火曜日ではありません。水曜日です。
Iie, Ka-yōbi dewa arimasen.[1] **Sui-yōbi desu.**
No, it's not Tuesday. It's Wednesday.

Brown   : 水曜日は何日ですか。
Sui-yōbi wa nan-nichi desu ka?
What day is Wednesday?

Kimura : 六日です。
Muika desu.
It's the 6th.

 POINTS TO REMEMBER

1. A **wa** B **dewa arimasen**: A is not B
   Dewa arimasen is the negative of **desu**.
   > EXAMPLE: 今日は火曜日ではありません。
   > **Kyō wa Ka-yōbi dewa arimasen.**
   > *Today is not Tuesday.*

   A **wa** B **dewa arimasen deshita**: A was not B
   Dewa arimasen deshita is the past negative of **desu**.
   > きのうは休みではありませんでした。
   > **Kinō wa yasumi dewa arimasen deshita.**
   > *Yesterday was not a holiday.*

ADDITIONAL WORDS

Study these new words and clearly pronounce them aloud. Then proceed to the exercises.

日曜日	**Nichi-yōbi**	*Sunday*
月曜日	**Getsu-yōbi***	*Monday*
火曜日	**Ka-yōbi***	*Tuesday*
水曜日	**Sui-yōbi***	*Wednesday*
木曜日	**Moku-yōbi**	*Thursday*
金曜日	**Kin-yōbi**	*Friday*
土曜日	**Do-yōbi**	*Saturday*
今週	**kon-shū**	*this week*
週	**-shū**	*week*
来週	**rai-shū**	*next week*
先週	**sen-shū**	*last week*
休み	**yasumi**	*holiday; non-working day*
買い物	**kaimono**	*shopping*
展覧会	**tenran-kai**	*exhibition*

* These words appear in the dialogue.

EXERCISES

A. Practice saying the following sentences in Japanese. Repeat the exercises until you no longer need to refer to the Japanese half.

1. *What day of the week is today?* **Kyō wa nan-yōbi desu ka?** 今日は何曜日です か。

   What day of the week is tomorrow? **Ashita wa nan-yōbi desu ka?** あしたは何曜日で すか。

   What day of the week is (for) shopping? **Kaimono wa nan-yōbi desu ka?** 買い物は何曜日 ですか。

   What day of the week is Mr. Yamada's farewell party? **Yamada-san no sōbetsu-kai wa nan-yōbi desu ka?** 山田さんの送別会 は何曜日ですか。

2. *What day of the week was yesterday?* **Kino wa nan-yōbi deshita ka?** きのうは何曜日 でしたか。

   What day of the week was the exhibition? **Tenran-kai wa nan-yōbi deshita ka?** 展覧会は何曜日 でしたか。

   What day of the week was the conference? **Kaigi wa nan-yōbi deshita ka?** 会議は何曜日でし たか。

3. *Today is Monday.* **Kyō wa Getsu-yōbi desu.** 今日は月曜日です。

   Today is Wednesday. **Kyō wa Sui-yōbi desu.** 今日は水曜日 です。

   Today is Friday. **Kyō wa Kin-yōbi desu.** 今日は金曜日 です。

4. *Yesterday was Sunday.* **Kinō wa Nichi-yōbi deshita.** きのうは日曜日 でした。

   Yesterday was a holiday. **Kinō wa yasumi deshita.** きのうは休み でした。

   Yesterday was Tuesday. **Kinō wa Ka-yōbi deshita.** きのうは火曜日 でした。

5. | *Mr. Tanaka's farewell party is this week/ next week.* | **Tanaka-san no sōbetsu-kai wa kon-shū/rai-shū desu.** | 田中さんの送別会は今週／来週です。 |
|---|---|---|
| *Mr. Tanaka's farewell party is Thursday of this week.* | **Tanaka-san no sōbetsu-kai wa kon-shū no Moku-yōbi desu.** | 田中さんの送別会は今週の木曜日です。 |
| *Mr. Tanaka's farewell party is Saturday of next week.* | **Tanaka-san no sōbetsu-kai wa rai-shū no Do-yōbi desu.** | 田中さんの送別会は来週の土曜日です。 |

6. | *Today is not Tuesday.* | **Kyō wa Ka-yōbi dewa arimasen.** | 今日は火曜ではありません。 |
|---|---|---|
| *Today is not the 5th.* | **Kyō wa itsuka dewa arimasen.** | 今日は五日ではありません。 |
| *Today is not Miss Tanaka's wedding.* | **Kyō wa Tanaka-san no kekkon-shiki dewa arimasen.** | 今日は田中さんの結婚式ではありません。 |

7. | *Yesterday was not a holiday.* | **Kinō wa yasumi dewa arimasen deshita.** | きのうは休みではありませんでした。 |
|---|---|---|
| *Yesterday was not my birthday.* | **Kinō wa watashi no tanjō-bi dewa arimasen deshita.** | きのうは私の誕生日ではありませんでした。 |
| *Yesterday was not Mr. Kimura's graduation.* | **Kinō wa Kimura-san no sotsugyō-shiki dewa arimasen deshita.** | きのうは木村さんの卒業式ではありませんでした。 |

B. Answer the following questions using the cue words.

1. **Kyō wa nan-yōbi desu ka?**
今日は何曜日ですか。
(Tuesday) ——————————————————————————

2. **Kinō wa yasumi deshita ka?**
きのうは休みでしたか。
Iie, ————————————————————————————

3. **Yamada-san no sōbetsu-kai wa nan-yōbi desu ka?**
山田さんの送別会は何曜日ですか。
(Wednesday of next week) ——————————————————

4. **Tsugi no yasumi wa Getsu-yōbi desu ka?**
   次の休みは月曜日ですか。
   Iie, _____

5. **Sen-shū no Do-yōbi wa nan-nichi deshita ka?**
   先週の土曜日は何日でしたか。
   (6th) _____

6. **Kaimono wa nan-yōbi desu ka?**
   買い物は何曜日ですか。
   (Saturday of this week) _____

ANSWERS

B.
1. **Kyō wa Ka-yōbi desu.** 今日は火曜日です。
2. **Iie, (kinō wa) yasumi dewa arimasen deshita.**
   いいえ、(きのうは)休みではありませんでした。
3. **(Yamada-san no sōbetsu-kai wa) rai-shū no Sui-yōbi desu.**
   (山田さんの送別会は)来週の水曜日です。
4. **Iie, Getsu-yōbi dewa arimasen.** いいえ、月曜日ではありません。
5. **Muika deshita.** 六日でした。
6. **Kon-shū no Do-yōbi desu.** 今週の土曜日です。

When Is Your Trip?

VOCABULARY

Study these words and clearly pronounce them aloud. Then proceed to
the dialogue.

いい	**ii**	*good*
暖かい	**atatakai**	*warm*
天気	**tenki**	*weather*
旅行	**ryokō**	*trip; travel*
加藤	**Katō**	(a family name)
一人	**hitori**	*alone*
友達	**tomodachi**	*friend*
と一緒	**to issho**[2]	*together with*
いつ	**itsu**	*when*
今月	**kon-getsu**[1]	*this month*
月	**-getsu**	*month*
来月	**rai-getsu**	*next month*
五月	**Go-gatsu**[1]	*May*
月	**-gatsu**	(a suffix used for the names of the months)

DIALOGUE

Study the dialogue below. Practice until you no longer need to refer to the
Japanese half.

Katō : 今日はいい天気ですね。
　　　 Kyō wa ii tenki desu ne.
　　　 Today is good weather, isn't it?
Baker : 暖かいですね。
　　　 Atatakai desu ne.
　　　 Warm, isn't it?
Katō : あなたの旅行はいつですか。今月ですか。
　　　 Anata no ryokō wa itsu desu ka? Kon-getsu[1] **desu ka?**
　　　 When is your trip? Is it this month?

Baker : いいえ、来月です。五月です。
　　　　Iie, rai-getsu¹ desu. Go-gatsu¹ desu.
　　　　No. It's next month. It's (in) May.
Katō : 一人ですか。
　　　　Hitori desu ka?
　　　　Will you be (go) alone?
Baker : いいえ、友達と一緒です。
　　　　Iie, tomodachi to issho desu.
　　　　No. I will be with a friend.

 POINTS TO REMEMBER

1. While the names of the months use **-gatsu**, such as **Go-gatsu** (May), "this month" and "next month" use **-getsu**.

2. NOUN + **to issho**: together with NOUN
　　EXAMPLE: 田中さんと一緒です。
　　　　　　Tanaka-san to issho desu.
　　　　　　I'll be with Mr. Tanaka.

ADDITIONAL WORDS
Included here are the names of the months. Study all of this list and clearly pronounce each word aloud. Then proceed to the exercises.

一月	**Ichi-gatsu**	*January*
二月	**Ni-gatsu**	*February*
三月	**San-gatsu**	*March*
四月	**Shi-gatsu**	*April*
五月	**Go-gatsu***	*May*
六月	**Roku-gatsu**	*June*
七月	**Shichi-gatsu**	*July*
八月	**Hachi-gatsu**	*August*
九月	**Ku-gatsu**	*September*
十月	**Jū-gatsu**	*October*
十一月	**Jū-ichi-gatsu**	*November*
十二月	**Jū-ni-gatsu**	*December*
先月	**sen-getsu**	*last month*
暑い	**atsui**	*hot*
寒い	**samui**	*cold*
涼しい	**suzushii**	*cool*
悪い	**warui**	*bad*

父	**chichi**	(*my*) *father* (used to refer to one's own father when talking to non-family persons)
お父さん	**o-tō-san** (polite)	*someone else's father; Father!* (used to refer to someone else's father, or when directly addressing one's own father)
母	**haha**	(*my*) *mother*
お母さん	**o-kā-san** (polite)	*someone else's mother; Mother!*

* This word appears in the dialogue.

EXERCISES

A. Practice saying the following sentences in Japanese. Repeat the exercises until you no longer need to refer to the Japanese half.

1.
Today is good weather, isn't it?	**Kyō wa ii tenki desu ne.**	今日はいい天気ですね。
Today is bad weather, isn't it?	**Kyō wa warui tenki desu ne.**	今日は悪い天気ですね。
Today is warm, isn't it?	**Kyō wa atatakai desu ne.**	今日は暖かいですね。
Today is hot, isn't it?	**Kyō wa atsui desu ne.**	今日は暑いですね。
Today is cool, isn't it?	**Kyō wa suzushii desu ne.**	今日は涼しいですね。
Today is cold, isn't it?	**Kyō wa samui desu ne.**	今日は寒いですね。

2.
When is your trip?	**Anata no ryokō wa itsu desu ka?**	あなたの旅行はいつですか。
It's this month.	**Kon-getsu desu.**	今月です。
It's next month.	**Rai-getsu desu.**	来月です。
It's (in) March.	**San-gatsu desu.**	三月です。
It's (in) May.	**Go-gatsu desu.**	五月です。
It's (in) October.	**Jū-gatsu desu.**	十月です。

3. *Today is January 3rd.* **Kyō wa Ichi-gatsu mikka desu.** 今日は一月三日 です。

   Today is June 20th. **Kyō wa Roku-gatsu hatsuka desu.** 今日は六月二十日 です。

   Today is July 4th. **Kyō wa Shichi-gatsu yokka desu.** 今日は七月四日で す。

   Today is December 25th. **Kyō wa Jū-ni-gatsu ni-jū-go-nichi desu.** 今日は十二月二十 五日です。

4. *When was Mr. Sato's graduation?* **Satō-san no sotsugyō-shiki wa itsu deshita ka?** 佐藤さんの卒業式 はいつでしたか。

   It was April 14th. **Shi-gatsu jū-yokka deshita.** 四月十四日でした。

   It was September 7th. **Ku-gatsu nanoka deshita.** 九月七日でした。

   It was the 12th of last month. **Sen-getsu no jū-ni-nichi deshita.** 先月の十二日でし た。

5. *I will be alone.* **Watashi wa hitori desu.** 私は一人です。

   I will be with a friend. **Watashi wa tomodachi to issho desu.** 私は友達と一緒 です。

   I will be with my father. **Watashi wa chichi to issho desu.** 私は父と一緒です。

   I will be with my mother. **Watashi wa haha to issho desu.** 私は母と一緒です。

   I will be with Miss Toda's father. **Watashi wa Toda-san no o-tō-san to issho desu.** 私は戸田さんの お父さんと一緒 です。

   I will be with Mr. Sato's mother. **Watashi wa Satō-san no o-kā-san to issho desu.** 私は佐藤さんの お母さんと一緒 です。

B. Answer the following questions using the cue words.

1. **Shi-gatsu wa atatakai desu ka?**
   四月は暖かいですか。
   Hai, _____

2. **Anata no tanjō-bi wa itsu desu ka?**
   あなたの誕生日はいつですか。
   (April 18th) _____

3. **Kimura-san no ryokō wa itsu desu ka?**
   木村さんの旅行はいつですか。
   (next month) _____

4. **Kimura-san wa hitori desu ka?**
   木村さんは一人ですか。
   (with a friend) _____

   (with his father) _____

5. **Tanaka-san no kekkon-shiki wa itsu deshita ka?**
   田中さんの結婚式はいつでしたすか。
   (6th of last month) _____

6. **Ichi-gatsu wa samui desa ka?**
   一月は寒いですか。
   Hai, _____

7. **Kinō wa ii tenki deshita ka?**
   きのうはいい天気でしたか。
   Iie, _____

ANSWERS

B.

1. **Hai, atatakai desu.** はい、暖かいです。
2. **Shi-gatsu jū-hachi-nichi desu.** 四月十八日です。
3. **Rai-getsu desu.** 来月です。
4. **Iie, tomodachi to issho desu.** いいえ、友達と一緒です。
   Iie, o-tō-san to issho desu. いいえ、お父さんと一緒です。
5. **Sen-getsu no muika deshita.** 先月の六日でした。
6. **Hai, samui desu.** はい、寒いです。
7. **Iie, warui tenki deshita.** いいえ、悪い天気でした。

Is There a Restaurant?

VOCABULARY

Study these words and clearly pronounce them aloud. Then proceed to the dialogue.

に	**ni**[1]	*at; in; on* (a location marker)
が	**ga**[2]	(a subject marker)
レストラン	**resutoran**	*restaurant*
五階	**go-kai**	*the 5th floor*
階	**-kai**	(a suffix used for floors)
天ぷら	**tenpura**	*Japanese deep-fried food*
エビ	**ebi**	*shrimp*
お飲物	**o-nomimono**	*a drink*
ビール	**biiru**	*beer*
あります	**arimasu**[3]	*exist; there is/are* (for inanimate objects)
ございます	**gozaimasu** (polite)	*exist; there is/are* (for inanimate objects)
何の	**nan no**[4]	*what kind of*
お願いします。	**O-negai shimasu.**	*Please.* (*lit.*, I make a request)
お願い	**o-negai**	*request*
かしこまりました。	**Kashikomarimashita.**	*Certainly, sir/ma'am.* (This expression is used when addressing one's employer or customer, and means "I'll do as you have requested.")

DIALOGUE

Study the dialogue below. Practice until you no longer need to refer to the Japanese half.

Tourist　：このホテルにレストランがありますか。

Kono hoteru ni¹ resutoran ga² arimasu ka?³

Is there a restaurant in this hotel?

Clerk　：はい、五階にございます。

Hai, go-kai ni gozaimasu.

Yes. There is (one) on the 5th floor.

* * * * * *

Tourist　：天ぷら、お願いします。

Tenpura, o-negai shimasu.

Tenpura, please.

Waitress　：何の天ぷらですか。

Nan no⁴ tenpura desu ka?

What kind of tenpura?

Tourist　：エビの天ぷらです。

Ebi no tenpura desu.

Shrimp tenpura.

Waitress　：お飲物は。

O-nomimono wa?⁵

How about a drink?

Tourist　：ビール、お願いします。

Biiru, o-negai shimasu.

Beer, please.

Waitress　：かしこまりました。

Kashikomarimashita.

Certainly, sir.

POINTS TO REMEMBER

1. NOUN + **ni**: at/in/on NOUN

   Ni is added to a noun and indicates the location of something.

   EXAMPLE: ホテルに本屋があります。

   Hoteru ni hon-ya ga arimasu.

   There is a bookshop in the hotel.

   Ni has other functions which will be discussed in Lessons 13, 15, 17, 19, and 21.

2. NOUN + **ga**

   Ga is a subject marker indicating that the preceding noun is a subject of the sentence.

   > EXAMPLE: レストランがあります。
   >
   > **Resutoran ga arimasu.**
   >
   > *There is a restaurant./A restaurant exists.*

   Wa also indicates the subject of a sentence, but in these cases, the subject preceding **wa** is the topic of the sentence—thus, **wa** can be translated "as for ~."

   > EXAMPLE: 本があります。
   >
   > **Hon ga arimasu.**
   >
   > *There is a book.*
   >
   > 本は私の(本)です。
   >
   > **Hon wa watashi no (hon) desu.**
   >
   > *As for the book, it is mine.*

3. NOUN + **ga arimasu ka?**: Is/Are there NOUN?

   > EXAMPLE: 駅に電話がありますか。
   >
   > **Eki ni denwa ga arimasu ka?**
   >
   > *Is there a telephone at the station?*

4. **Nan no** + NOUN: what kind of NOUN

   > EXAMPLE: 何の雑誌ですか。
   >
   > **Nan no zasshi desu ka?**
   >
   > *What kind of magazine is it?*

5. The **wa** as used here turns the phrase into a question.

ADDITIONAL WORDS

Study these new words and clearly pronounce them aloud. Then proceed to the exercises.

カメラ屋	**kamera-ya**	*camera shop*
喫茶店	**kissaten**	*coffee shop*
旅行代理店	**ryokō-dairiten**	*travel agency*
地下	**chika**	*basement*
マグロ	**maguro**	*tuna*
刺身	**sashimi**	*sliced raw fish*
マグロの刺身	**maguro no sashimi**	*sliced raw tuna*
酒	**sake**	*Japanese rice wine*
ワイン	**wain**	*wine*
写真	**shashin**	*photo*

| 雑誌 | **zasshi** | *magazine* |
| スポーツ | **supōtsu** | *sport* |

EXERCISES

A. Practice saying the following sentences in Japanese. Repeat the exercises until you no longer need to refer to the Japanese half.

1. *Is there a restaurant in this hotel?* **Kono hoteru ni resutoran ga arimasu ka?** このホテルにレストランがありますか。

   Is there a coffee shop in this hotel? **Kono hoteru ni kissaten ga arimasu ka?** このホテルに喫茶店がありますか。

   Is there a camera shop in this hotel? **Kono hoteru ni kamera-ya ga arimasu ka?** このホテルにカメラ屋がありますか。

   Is there a travel agency in this hotel? **Kono hoteru ni ryokō-dairiten ga arimasu ka?** このホテルに旅行代理店がありますか。

2. *Yes, there is (one) on the 5th floor.* **Hai, go-kai ni gozaimasu.** はい、五階にございます。

   Yes, there is (one) on the 7th floor. **Hai, nana-kai ni gozaimasu.** はい、七階にございます。

   Yes, there is (one) in the basement. **Hai, chika ni gozaimasu.** はい、地下にございます。

3. *Tenpura, please.* **Tenpura, o-negai shimasu.** 天ぷら、お願いします。

   Sashimi, please. **Sashimi, o-negai shimasu.** 刺身、お願いします。

   Beer, please. **Biiru, o-negai shimasu.** ビール、お願いします。

   Wine, please. **Wain, o-negai shimasu.** ワイン、お願いします。

   Sake, please. **Sake, o-negai shimasu.** 酒、お願いします。

4. *What kind of tenpura is it?* **Nan no tenpura desu ka?** 何の天ぷらですか。

   What kind of sashimi is it? **Nan no sashimi desu ka?** 何の刺身ですか。

What kind of photo is it?	**Nan no shashin desu ka?**	何の写真ですか。
What kind of magazine is it?	**Nan no zasshi desu ka?**	何の雑誌ですか。

5. *It's shrimp tempura.*   **Ebi no tenpura desu.**   エビの天ぷらです。

   It's tuna sashimi.   **Maguro no sashimi desu.**   マグロの刺身です。

   It's a sport magazine.   **Supōtsu no zasshi desu.**   スポーツの雑誌です。

   It's a photo magazine.   **Shashin no zasshi desu.**   写真の雑誌です。

B. Answer the following questions using the cue words.

1. **Kono hoteru ni ryokō-dairiten ga arimasu ka?**
   このホテルに旅行代理店がありますか。
   (in the basement) **Hai, _____ gozaimasu.**

2. **Kono depāto ni kissaten ga arimasu ka?**
   このデパートに喫茶店がありますか。
   (on the 5th floor) **Hai, _____ .**

3. **Kono tatemono ni kamera-ya ga arimasu ka?**
   この建物にカメラ屋がありますか。
   (on the 7th floor) **Hai, _____ .**

C. Order the following items:

1. beer   2. shrimp tempura   3. sliced raw tuna   4. Wine

ANSWERS

B.
1. **Hai, chika ni gozaimasu.** はい、地下にございます。
2. **Hai, go-kai ni gozaimasu.** はい、五階にございます。
3. **Hai, nana-kai ni gozaimasu.** はい、七階にございます。

C.
1. **Biiru, o-negai shimasu.** ビールお願いします。
2. **Ebi no tenpura, o-negai shimasu.** エビの天ぷらお願いします。
3. **Maguro no sashimi, o-negai shimasu.** マグロの刺身お願いします。
4. **Wain, o-negai shimasu.** ワインお願いします。

How Many Tables Are There?

VOCABULARY

Study these words and clearly pronounce them aloud. Then proceed to the dialogue.

太田	**Ōta**	(a family name)
部屋	**heya**	*room*
会議室	**kaigi-shitsu**	*conference room*
テーブル	**tēburu**	*table*
椅子	**isu**	*chair*
灰皿	**haizara**	*ashtray*
マッチ	**matchi**	*match*
いくつ	**ikutsu**[1]	*how many* (things)
二つ	**futatsu**	*two*
四つ	**yottsu**	*four*
十	**tō**	*ten*
ありません	**arimasen**[2]	*do not exist; there is/are not*

DIALOGUE

Study the dialogue below. Practice until you no longer need to refer to the Japanese half.

Hart : あの部屋はなんですか。
Ano heya wa nan desu ka?
What is that room?

Ōta : 会議室です。
Kaigi-shitsu desu.
It's a conference room.

Hart : 会議室にテーブルがいくつありますか。
Kaigi-shitsu ni tēburu ga ikutsu[1] arimasu ka?
How many tables are there in the conference room?

Ōta : 二つあります。
Futatsu arimasu.
There are two.

Hart : 椅子がいくつありますか。
Isu ga ikutsu arimasu ka?
How many chairs are there?

Ōta : 十あります。
Tō arimasu.
There are ten.

Hart : 灰皿がありますか。
Haizara ga arimasu ka?
Are there ashtrays?

Ōta : はい、四つあります。
Hai, yottsu arimasu.
Yes, there are four.

Hart : マッチは。
Matchi wa?
How about matches?

Ōta : マッチはありません。
Matchi wa arimasen.[2]
There are no matches.

📖 POINTS TO REMEMBER

1. **NOUN + ga + ikutsu arimasu ka?**: How many NOUN are there?
   EXAMPLE: 椅子がいくつありますか。
   Isu ga ikutsu arimasu ka?
   How many chairs are there?

2. **NOUN + wa arimasen**: There is/are no NOUN
   Wa is frequently used in negative sentences to contrast a negative idea with a positive idea.
   EXAMPLE: 灰皿があります。マッチはありません。
   Haizara ga arimasu. Matchi wa arimasen.
   There are ashtrays. [But] *There are no matches.*

ADDITIONAL WORDS

The Japanese language has two sets of numerals: the regular numbers, **ichi**, **ni**, **san**, etc., that were introduced in Lesson 4, and another set shown below. For counting objects, use this new set of numbers (**hitotsu**, **futatsu**, **mittsu**, etc.,) when indicating one through ten, and then continue with the regular numbers when indicating eleven and above.

Study these words and clearly pronounce them aloud. Then proceed to the exercises.

一つ	**hitotsu**	*one*
二つ	**futatsu***	*two*
三つ	**mittsu**	*three*
四つ	**yottsu***	*four*
五つ	**itsutsu**	*five*
六つ	**muttsu**	*six*
七つ	**nanatsu**	*seven*
八つ	**yattsu**	*eight*
九つ	**kokonotsu**	*nine*
十	**tō***	*ten*
〜の上に	**~ no ue ni**	*on top of ~*
〜の中に	**~ no naka ni**	*in/inside ~*
箱	**hako**	*box*
コップ	**koppu**	*cup; glass*
リンゴ	**ringo**	*apple*
机	**tsukue**	*desk*

* These words appear in the dialogue.

EXERCISES

A. Practice saying the following sentences in Japanese. Repeat the exercises until you no longer need to refer to the Japanese half.

1. *How many tables are there in the room?*
   Heya ni tēburu ga ikutsu arimasu ka?
   部屋にテーブルがいくつありますか。

There are two.	**Futatsu arimasu.**	二つあります。
There are four.	**Yottsu arimasu.**	四つあります。
There is one.	**Hitotsu arimasu.**	一つあります。

2. *How many chairs are there in the conference room?*
Kaigi-shitsu ni isu ga ikutsu arimasu ka?
会議室に椅子がいくつありますか。

There are seven.	**Nanatsu arimasu.**	七つあります。
There are nine.	**Kokonotsu arimasu.**	九つあります。
There are twelve.	**Jū-ni arimasu.**	十二あります。

3. *How many ashtrays are there on the desk?*
Tsukue no ue ni haizara ga ikutsu arimasu ka?
机の上に灰皿がいくつありますか。

There are three.	**Mittsu arimasu.**	三つあります。
There are six.	**Muttsu arimasu.**	六つあります。
There are ten.	**Tō arimasu.**	十あります。

4. *How many apples are there in the box?*
Hako no naka ni ringo ga ikutsu arimasu ka?
箱の中にリンゴがいくつありますか。

There are five.	**Itsutsu arimasu.**	五つあります。
There are eight.	**Yattsu arimasu.**	八つあります。
There are twenty.	**Ni-jū arimasu.**	二十あります。

5. | *There are no magazines.* | **Zasshi wa arimasen.** | 雑誌はありません。 |
|---|---|---|
| *There are no ashtrays.* | **Haizara wa arimasen.** | 灰皿はありません。 |
| *There are no matches.* | **Matchi wa arimasen.** | マッチはありません。 |

B. Answer the following questions using the cue words.

1. **Tēburu no ue ni ringo ga ikutsu arimasu ka?**
テーブルの上にリンゴがいくつありますか。
(seven) _____

2. **Haizara ga ikutsu arimasu ka?**
灰皿がいくつありますか。
(eight) _____

3. **Matchi wa?**
   マッチは？
   (none) _____

4. **Kaigi-shitsu ni isu ga ikutsu arimasu ka?**
   会議室に椅子がいくつありますか。
   (twelve) _____

5. **Tsukue no ue ni koppu ga ikutsu arimasu ka?**
   机の上にコップがいくつありますか。
   (three) _____

6. **Hako no naka ni ringo ga ikutsu arimasu ka?**
   箱の中にリンゴがいくつありますか。
   (twenty) _____

ANSWERS

B.
1. **Nanatsu arimasu.** 七つあります。
2. **Yattsu arimasu.** 八つあります。
3. **Matchi wa arimasen.** マッチはありません。
4. **Jū-ni arimasu.** 十二あります。
5. **Mittsu arimasu.** 三つあります。
6. **Ni-jū arimasu.** 二十あります。

LESSON 11

How Many Persons Are There?

VOCABULARY

Study these words and clearly pronounce them aloud. Then proceed to the dialogue.

男の人	**otoko no hito**	*a man*
男	**otoko**	*male* (*person*)
女の人	**onna no hito**	*a woman*
女	**onna**	*female* (*person*)
秘書	**hisho**	*secretary*
営業部	**eigyō-bu**	*sales department*
何人	**nan-nin**	*how many persons*
人	**-nin**	(a suffix used for persons)
六人	**roku-nin**	*6 persons*
九人	**ku-nin**	*9 persons*
十五人	**jū-go-nin**	*15 persons*
みんな	**minna**	*all*
若い	**wakai**	*young*
います	**imasu**[1]	*exist; there is/are* (for animate objects)

DIALOGUE

Study the dialogue below. Practice until you no longer need to refer to the Japanese half.

Hart : あそこはなんですか。
Asoko wa nan desu ka?
What is that over there?

Ōta : あそこですか。営業部です。
Asoko desu ka? Eigyō-bu desu.
That over there? It's the sales department.

Hart : あの部屋に人が何人いますか。
Ano heya ni hito ga nan-nin imasu ka?[1]
How many persons are there in that room?

Ōta : 十五人います。男の人が九人います。女の人が六人います。
Jū-go-nin imasu. Otoko no hito ga ku-nin imasu. Onna no hito ga roku-nin imasu.
There are fifteen people. There are nine men. There are six women.

Hart : 秘書がいますか。
Hisho ga imasu ka?
Is there a secretary?

Ōta : はい、います。若い女の人です。女の人はみんな若いです。
Hai, imasu. Wakai onna no hito desu. Onna no hito wa minna wakai desu.
Yes, there is. She is a young woman. The women are all young.

 POINTS TO REMEMBER

1. NOUN + **ga** + **nan-nin imasu ka?** How many NOUN are there?
   EXAMPLE: 女の人が何人いますか。
   Onna no hito ga nan-nin imasu ka?
   How many women are there?

ADDITIONAL WORDS

Study these people-related words and clearly pronounce them aloud. Then proceed to the exercises.

Persons (-nin)

一人	**hitori**	*1 person*
二人	**futari**	*2 persons*
三人	**san-nin**	*3 persons*
四人	**yo-nin**	*4 persons*
五人	**go-nin**	*5 persons*
六人	**roku-nin***	*6 persons*
七人	**shichi-nin/nana-nin**	*7 persons*
八人	**hachi-nin**	*8 persons*
九人	**ku-nin*/kyū-nin**	*9 persons*
十人	**jū-nin**	*10 persons*
十一人	**jū-ichi-nin**	*11 persons*
四十人	**yon-jū-nin**	*40 persons*
九十人	**kyū-jū-nin**	*90 persons*
百人	**hyaku-nin**	*100 persons*
たくさん	**takusan**	*many (people/things)*
いません	**imasen**	*do not exist; there is/are not (used for animate objects)*

* These words appear in the dialogue.

EXERCISES

A. Practice saying the following sentences in Japanese. Repeat the exercises until you no longer need to refer to the Japanese half.

1. *How many persons are there in the company?* — **Kaisha ni hito ga nan-nin imasu ka?** — 会社に人が何人いますか。

   How many persons are there in the sales department? — **Eigyō-bu ni hito ga nan-nin imasu ka?** — 営業部に人が何人いますか。

   How many persons are there in the conference room? — **Kaigi-shitsu ni hito ga nan-nin imasu ka?** — 会議室に人が何人いますか。

2. *How many persons are there in that room?* — **Ano heya ni hito ga nan-nin imasu ka?** — あの部屋に人が何人いますか。

   There are fifteen. — **Jū-go-nin imasu.** — 十五人います。

   There are twenty-six. — **Ni-jū-roku-nin imasu.** — 二十六人います。

   There are many. — **Takusan imasu.** — たくさんいます。

3. *How many men are there in the sales department?* — **Eigyō-bu ni otoko no hito ga nan-nin imasu ka?** — 営業部に男の人が何人いますか。

   There are nine. — **Ku-nin/Kyū-nin imasu.** — 九人います。

   There are seven. — **Nana-nin/Shichi-nin imasu.** — 七人います。

   There are about ten. — **Jū-nin gurai imasu.** — 十人ぐらいいます。

4. *How many women are there in the restaurant?* — **Resutoran ni onna no hito ga nan-nin imasu ka?** — レストランに女の人が何人いますか。

   There are two. — **Futari imasu.** — 二人います。

   There are eight. — **Hachi-nin imasu.** — 八人います。

   There are about fourteen. — **Jū-yo-nin gurai imasu.** — 十四人ぐらいいます。

5. *There are no secretaries.* — **Hisho wa imasen.** — 秘書はいません。

   There are no young men. — **Wakai otoko no hito wa imasen.** — 若い男の人はいません。

   There are no good doctors. — **Ii isha wa imasen.** — いい医者はいません。

6. *The reporters are all good.*   **Kisha wa minna ii desu.**   記者はみんな
いいです。

The teachers are all young.   **Sensei wa minna wakai desu.**   先生はみんな
若いです。

B. Answer the following questions using the cue words.

1. **Anata no kaisha ni hito ga nan-nin imasu ka?**
あなたの会社に人が何人いますか。
(about one hundred) _____

2. **Kaigi-shitsu ni otoko no hito ga nan-nin imasu ka?**
会議室に男の人が何人いますか。
(eight) _____

3. **Onna no hito wa?**
女の人は？
(none) _____

4. **Eigyō-bu ni hisho ga nan-nin imasu ka?**
営業部に秘書が何人いますか。
(one) _____

5. **Ano heya ni sensei ga nan-nin imasu ka?**
あの部屋に先生が何人いますか。
(about four) _____

6. **Sensei wa minna wakai desu ka?**
先生はみんな若いですか。
Hai, _____

ANSWERS

B.
1. **Hyaku-nin gurai imasu.** 百人ぐらいいます。
2. **Hachi-nin imasu.** 八人います。
3. **Imasen.** いません。
4. **Hitori imasu.** 一人います。
5. **Yo-nin gurai imasu.** 四人ぐらいいます。
6. **Hai, minna wakai desu.** はい、みんな若いです。

Review Exercises

The following sentences were covered in Lessons 1 through 11. Before proceeding to Lesson 13, repeat these practice sentences until you no longer need to refer to the Japanese half.

1. *Good morning.* **Ohayō gozaimasu.** おはようございます。
   How are you?/ **O-genki desu ka?** お元気ですか。
   Are you well?
   Yes, I'm fine. **Hai, genki desu.** はい、元気です。

2. *How do you do?* **Hajimemashite.** はじめまして。
   Glad to meet you. **Dōzo yoroshiku.** どうぞよろしく。

3. *Thank you.* **Dōmo arigatō.** どうもありがとう。
   You are welcome. **Dō-itashimashite.** どういたしまして。

4. *Please* (have some). **Dōzo.** どうぞ。
   I will have some. **Itadakimasu.** いただきます。
   It was delicious. **Gochisō-sama deshita.** ごちそうさまでした。

5. *Who is that person?* **Ano hito wa dare desu ka?** あの人は誰ですか。
   He is Mr. Yamada. **Yamada-san desu.** 山田さんです。

6. *Are you Mr. Carter?* **Anata wa Kātā-san desu ka?** あなたはカーターさんですか。
   Yes, I am. **Hai, Kātā desu.** はい、カーターです。

7. *Are you an American?* **Anata wa Amerika no kata desu ka?** あなたはアメリカの方ですか。
   Yes, I am an American. **Hai, watashi wa Amerika-jin desu.** はい、私はアメリカ人です。

8. *Is Miss Toda a teacher?*
Toda-san wa sensei desu ka?
戸田さんは先生
ですか。

No. She is a nurse.
Iie, (Toda-san wa) kangoshi desu.
いいえ、(戸田さん
は)看護師です。

9. *What is that building?*
Ano tatemono wa nan desu ka?
あの建物は何です
か。

That's the Imperial Hotel.
Are wa Teikoku Hoteru desu.
あれは帝国ホテル
です。

10. *Where is the post office?*
Yūbin-kyoku wa doko desu ka?
郵便局はどこです
か。

It's in front of the station.
Eki no mae desu.
駅の前です。

11. *What time is it now?*
Ima nan-ji desu ka?
今何時ですか。

It's 9:00.
Ku-ji desu.
九時です。

12. *What time is the next train?*
Tsugi no densha wa nan-ji desu ka?
次の電車は何時
ですか。

It's at 10:15.
Jū-ji jū-go-fun desu.
十時十五分です。

13. *What track is the train for Osaka?*
Ōsaka-yuki wa nan-ban-sen desu ka?
大阪行きは何番線
ですか。

It's track no. 6.
Roku-ban-sen desu.
6番線です。

14. *From here to the airport, how many hours is it?*
Koko kara kūkō made, nan-jikan desu ka?
ここから空港まで、
何時間ですか。

It's about one and a half hours.
Ichi-jikan-han gurai desu.
一時間半ぐらい
です。

15. *From the embassy to the library, how many minutes is it?*
Taishi-kan kara tosho-kan made nan-pun desu ka?
大使館から図書館
まで、何分ですか。

It's about 8 minutes by taxi.
Takushii de hachi-fun gurai desu.
タクシーで八分
ぐらいです。

16. *The concert is from 7 P.M. till 9:00.*
Konsāto wa gogo shichi-ji kara ku-ji made desu.
コンサートは午後
七時から九時まで
です。

17. *Is the Kabuki Theater near from here?* **Kabuki-za wa koko kara chikai desu ka?** 歌舞伎座はここから近いですか。
No. It's far. **Iie, tōi desu.** いいえ、遠いです。

18. *What's the date today?* **Kyō wa nan-nichi desu ka?** 今日は何日ですか。
It's the 5th. **Itsuka desu.** 五日です。

19. *Today is good weather, isn't it?* **Kyō wa ii tenki desu ne.** 今日はいい天気ですね。
Warm, isn't it? **Atatakai desu ne.** 暖かいですね。

20. *What date was your graduation?* **Anata no sotsugyō-shiki wa nan-nichi deshita ka?** あなたの卒業式は何日でしたか。
It was the 14th. **Jū-yokka deshita.** 十四日でした。

21. *What day of the week is Miss Toda's wedding?* **Toda-san no kekkon-shiki wa nan-yōbi desu ka?** 戸田さんの結婚式は何曜日ですか。
It's Wednesday of next week. **Rai-shū no Sui-yōbi desu.** 来週の水曜日です。

22. *Is Mr. Kimura's farewell party this week?* **Kimura-san no sōbetsu-kai wa kon-shū desu ka?** 木村さんの送別会は今週ですか。
No, it isn't this week. **Iie, kon-shū dewa arimasen.** いいえ、今週ではありません。

23. *When is your trip?* **Anata no ryokō wa itsu desu ka?** あなたの旅行はいつですか。
It's (in) June. **Roku-gatsu desu.** 六月です。

24. *Will you be (go) alone?* **Hitori desu ka?** 一人ですか。
No. I'll be with my mother. **Iie, haha to issho desu.** いいえ、母と一緒です。

25. *Is there a coffee shop in this department store?* **Kono depāto ni kissaten ga arimasu ka?** このデパートに喫茶店がありますか。
Yes, there is (one) on the 2nd floor. **Hai, ni-kai ni arimasu/gozaimasu.** はい、二階にあります／ございます。

26. *Sashimi, please.*   **Sashimi, o-negai shimasu.**   刺身、お願い します。

   What kind of sashimi?   **Nan no sashimi desu ka?**   何の刺身ですか。

   Tuna sashimi.   **Maguro no sashimi desu.**   マグロの刺身です。

27. *How many chairs are there in the conference room?*   **Kaigi-shitsu ni isu ga ikutsu arimasu ka?**   会議室に椅子が いくつありますか。

   There are nine.   **Kokonotsu arimasu.**   九つあります。

28. *Are there ashtrays on the table?*   **Tēburu no ue ni haizara ga arimasu ka?**   テーブルの上に灰 皿がありますか。

   No, there are none.   **Iie, haizara wa arimasen.**   いいえ、灰皿はあり ません。

29. *How many persons are there in that room?*   **Ano heya ni hito ga nan-nin imasu ka?**   あの部屋に人が何 人いますか。

   There are about twenty.   **Ni-jū-nin gurai imasu.**   二十人ぐらいいます。

30. *Is Miss Ota young?*   **Ōta-san wa wakai desu ka?**   太田さんは若い ですか。

   Yes, she is.   **Hai, wakai desu.**   はい、若いです。

31. *Is Mrs. Tanaka a good secretary?*   **Tanaka-san wa ii hisho desu ka?**   田中さんはいい秘 書ですか。

   Yes, she is.   **Hai, ii hisho desu.**   はい、いい秘書 です。

LESSON 13

Where Are You Going?

VOCABULARY

Study these words and clearly pronounce them aloud. Then proceed to the dialogue.

京都	**Kyōto**	*Kyoto* (old capital of Japan)
お寺	**o-tera**	*Buddhist temple*
それから	**sore-kara**	*after that; then*
へ	**e**[1]	*to* (place)
に	**ni**[3]	*at; on* (time)
で	**de**[4]	*at; in* (place)
を	**o**[5]	(an object marker)
行きます（行く）	**ikimasu**[2] **(iku)***	*go*
帰ります（帰る）	**kaerimasu (kaeru)***	*return*
泊まります（泊まる）	**tomarimasu (tomaru)***	*stay (at a hotel)*
泊まりません	**tomarimasen**[6]	*do not stay*
見ます（見る）	**mimasu (miru)***	*see; watch; look*
します（する）	**shimasu (suru)***	*do*

* The words within parentheses are the infinitive forms (also called the dictionary form) of the verbs. An explanation of verbs will follow on page 72.

DIALOGUE

Study the dialogue below. Practice until you no longer need to refer to the Japanese half.

Satō : あなたはあしたどこへいきますか。
   Anata wa ashita doko e[1] **ikimasu**[2] **ka?**
   Where are you going tomorrow?
Parker : 京都へ行きます。
   Kyōto e ikimasu.
   I am going to Kyōto.

Satō　：何時に行きますか。

Nan-ji ni³ ikimasu ka?

What time are you going?

Parker：午前九時に行きます。

Gozen ku-ji ni ikimasu.

I'm going at 9:00 A.M.

Satō　：京都で何をしますか。

Kyōto de⁴ nani o⁵ shimasu ka?

What are you going to do in Kyoto?

Parker：お寺を見ます。それから買い物をします。

O-tera o mimasu. Sore-kara, kaimono o shimasu.

I'll see temples. After that I'll do some shopping.

Satō　：ホテルに泊まりますか。

Hoteru ni tomarimasu ka?

Are you going to stay at a hotel?

Parker：いいえ、泊まりません。午後八時に帰ります。

Iie, tomarimasen.⁶ Gogo hachi-ji ni kaerimasu.

No, I won't stay. I'll return at 8:00 P.M.

 POINTS TO REMEMBER

1. NOUN + **e**: to NOUN

   E is used to indicate direction.

   EXAMPLE: 私は京都／銀行へ行きます。

   　　　　Watashi wa Kyōto/ginkō e ikimasu.

   　　　　I am going to Kyoto/the bank.

2. The **-masu** form of the verb is used for present and future tenses.

   EXAMPLE: 郵便局へ行きます。

   　　　　Yūbin-kyoku e ikimasu.

   　　　　I go/will go to the post office.

3. NOUN + **ni**: at/on NOUN

   Ni is added to a time-related noun and indicates a point in time.

   EXAMPLES: 八時に行きます。

   　　　　Hachi-ji ni ikimasu.

   　　　　I'll go at 8:00.

   　　　　土曜日に帰ります。

   　　　　Do-yōbi ni kaerimasu.

   　　　　I'll return on Saturday.

4. NOUN + **de**: at/in NOUN

   De is added to a place-related noun to indicate where an action takes place.

   > EXAMPLE: 部屋で食べます。
   >
   > **Heya de tabemasu.**
   >
   > *I eat in the room.*

5. NOUN + **o shimasu**: do/will do NOUN

   Used as an object marker, **o** is added to a noun that is the direct object of a verb.

   > EXAMPLE: 本を読みます。
   >
   > **Hon o yomimasu.**
   >
   > *I read a book.*

   Note that the **o** may change to **wa** in negative sentences.

   > EXAMPLE: 雑誌は読みません。
   >
   > **Zasshi wa yomimasen.**
   >
   > *I don't read magazines.*

6. The ending **-masen** indicates negation.

   > EXAMPLE: 買いません
   >
   > **kaimasen**
   >
   > *don't/won't buy*

ADDITIONAL WORDS

Study these new words and clearly pronounce them aloud. Then proceed to the exercises.

朝ご飯	**asa-gohan**	*breakfast*
朝	**asa**	*morning*
ご飯	**gohan**	*meal; cooked rice*
昼ご飯	**hiru-gohan**	*lunch*
昼	**hiru**	*noon; daytime*
晩ご飯	**ban-gohan**	*supper*
晩	**ban**	*evening; night*
紅茶	**kō-cha**	*black tea*
コーヒー	**kōhii**	*coffee*
お茶	**o-cha**	*green tea*
お土産	**o-miyage**	*souvenir*
美術館	**bijutsu-kan**	*art museum*
買います（買う）	**kaimasu (kau)**	*buy*
飲みます（飲む）	**nomimasu (nomu)**	*drink*
読みます（読む）	**yomimasu (yomu)**	*read*

起きます（起きる）	**okimasu (okiru)**	*get up*
寝ます（寝る）	**nemasu (neru)**	*sleep; go to bed*
食べます（食べる）	**tabemasu (taberu)**	*eat*

JAPANESE VERBS

Japanese verbs may be divided into three groups: regular, semi-regular, and irregular verbs. They can be recognized as follows:

1. The dictionary form of the regular verb has a *consonant*: *u* ending.

    EXAMPLES: 行く   **iku**   *(go)*
              読む   **yomu**   *(read)*

2. The dictionary form of the semi-regular verb has a *-eru* or *-iru* ending.

    EXAMPLES: 食べる   **taberu**   *(eat)*
              見る   **miru**   *(see; watch; look)*

3. There are only two irregular verbs. They are, in their dictionary forms, **kuru** *(come)* and **suru** *(do)*.

    In this book, regular, semi-regular, and irregular verbs are classified as Group 1, Group 2, and Group 3 respectively. The verbs used in this lesson fall into the groups as shown below.

GROUP 1	GROUP 2	GROUP 3
行く **iku** (*go*)	食べる **taberu** (*eat*)	する **suru** (*do*)
泊まる **tomaru** (*stay*)	寝る **neru** (*sleep*)	来る **kuru** (*come*)
飲む **nomu** (*drink*)	見る **miru** (*see*)	
読む **yomu** (*read*)	起きる **okiru** (*get up*)	
買う **ka(w)u*** (*buy*)		
帰る **kaeru**** (*return*)		

* In modern Japanese, *w* disappears before all vowels except *a*. This affects the negative form of verbs like **kau**, as discussed in Lesson 21.

** Some verbs ending with *-eru/-iru* belong to Group 1.

The V-masu form

The V-masu forms of verbs are made as follows:

1. Group 1 verbs
   Drop the *-u* ending from the dictionary form and add *i* plus *-masu*.
   EXAMPLES: 行く **iku**   + i + ます **masu** → 行きます
                                                    iki*masu*

   泊まる **tomaru** + i + ます **masu** → 泊まります
                                                  tomari*masu*

   飲む **nomu**   + i + ます **masu** → 飲みます
                                                  nomi*masu*

   読む **yomu**   + i + ます **masu** → 読みます
                                                  yomi*masu*

   買う **kau**   + i + ます **masu** → 買います
                                                  kai*masu*

   帰る **kaeru**   + i + ます **masu** → 帰ります
                                                  kaeri*masu*

2. Group 2 verbs
   Drop the *-ru* ending and add *-masu*.
   EXAMPLES: 食べる **taberu** + ます **masu** → 食べます **tabe*masu***
               寝る **neru**   + ます **masu** → 寝ます **ne*masu***
               見る **miru**   + ます **masu** → 見ます **mi*masu***
               起きる **okiru** + ます **masu** → 起きます **oki*masu***

3. Group 3 verbs
   EXAMPLES: する **suru**   →   します **shi*masu***
               来る **kuru**   →   来ます **ki*masu***

EXERCISES

A. Practice saying the following sentences in Japanese. Repeat the exercises until you no longer need to refer to the Japanese half.

1. *Where are you going tomorrow?* **Anata wa ashita doko e ikimasu ka?** あなたはあしたどこへいきますか。
   I'm going to Kyoto. **Kyōto e ikimasu.** 京都へ行きます。
   I'm going to the hospital. **Byōin e ikimasu.** 病院へ行きます。
   I'm going to the temple. **O-tera e ikimasu.** お寺へ行きます。
   I'm going to the art museum. **Bijutsu-kan e ikimasu.** 美術館へ行きます。

2. *What time are you going?* | **Nan-ji ni ikimasu ka?** | 何時に行きますか。
What time are you returning? | **Nan-ji ni kaerimasu ka?** | 何時に帰りますか。
What time are you getting up? | **Nan-ji ni okimasu ka?** | 何時に起きますか。
What time are you going to bed? | **Nan-ji ni nemasu ka?** | 何時に寝ますか。

3. *What will you do in Kyoto?* | **Kyōto de nani o shimasu ka?** | 京都で何をしますか。
What will you eat at the restaurant? | **Resutoran de nani o tabemasu ka?** | レストランで何を食べますか。
What will you see at the art museum? | **Bijutsu-kan de nani o mimasu ka?** | 美術館で何を見ますか。
What will you buy at the department store? | **Depāto de nani o kaimasu ka?** | デパートで何を買いますか。
What will you drink at the coffee shop? | **Kissaten de nani o nomimasu ka?** | 喫茶店で何を飲みますか。
What do you read in the room? | **Heya de nani o yomimasu ka?** | 部屋で何を読みますか。

4. *I'll do some shopping in Kyoto.* | **Kyōto de kaimono o shimasu.** | 京都で買い物をします。
I'll eat lunch at the restaurant. | **Resutoran de hiru-gohan o tabemasu.** | レストランで昼ご飯を食べます。
I'll see the photos at the art museum. | **Bijutsu-kan de shashin o mimasu.** | 美術館で写真を見ます。
I'll buy souvenirs at the department store. | **Depāto de o-miyage o kaimasu.** | デパートでお土産を買います。
I'll drink black tea at the coffee shop. | **Kissaten de kō-cha o nomimasu.** | 喫茶店で紅茶を飲みます。
I'll read a newspaper in the room. | **Heya de shinbun o yomimasu.** | 部屋で新聞を読みます。

5. *I don't eat breakfast.* | **Asa-gohan wa tabemasen.** | 朝ご飯は食べません。
I don't drink coffee. | **Kōhii wa nomimasen.** | コーヒーは飲みません。
I won't stay at a hotel. | **Hoteru ni tomarimasen.** | ホテルに泊まりません。
I won't return to Tokyo. | **Tōkyō e kaerimasen.** | 東京へ帰りません。

B. Answer the following questions using the cue words.

1. **Anata wa doko e ikimasu ka?**
あなたはどこへ行きますか。
(temple) _____

2. **Depāto de nani o kaimasu ka?**
デパートで何を買いますか。
(souvenirs) _____

3. **Nan-ji ni ban-gohan o tabemasu ka?**
何時に晩ご飯を食べますか。
(6:30 P.M.) _____

4. **Doko de shashin o mimasu ka?**
どこで写真を見ますか。
(art museum) _____

5. **Hoteru ni tomarimasu ka?**
ホテルに泊まりますか。
Iie, _____

6. **Heya de o-cha o nomimasu ka?**
部屋でお茶を飲みますか。
Iie, _____

ANSWERS

B.
1. **O-tera e ikimasu.** お寺へ行きます。
2. **O-miyage o kaimasu.** お土産を買います。
3. **Gogo roku-ji-han ni tabemasu.** 午後六時半に食べます。
4. **Bijutsu-kan de mimasu.** 美術館で見ます。
5. **Iie, tomarimasen.** いいえ、泊まりません。
6. **Iie, nomimasen.** いいえ、飲みません。

LESSON 14

How Much Is This Vase?

VOCABULARY

Study these words and clearly pronounce them aloud. Then proceed to the dialogue.

いらしゃいませ。	**Irasshaimase.**	*Welcome.* (used for greeting customers entering a store, hotel, etc., and also for welcoming guests to your home)
花びん	**kabin**	*vase*
見せて下さい	**misete kudasai**	*please show*
見せる	**miseru**	*to show*
下さい	**kudasai**	*please; please give (me)*
青い	**aoi**	*blue*
青いの	**aoi-no**[1]	*blue one*
大きい	**ōkii**	*big*
ちょっと	**chotto**	*a little*
もっと	**motto**	*more*
小さいの	**chiisai-no**	*small one*
もっと小さいの	**motto chiisai-no**	*smaller one*
いかが	**ikaga**	*how (about)*
いくら	**ikura**	*how much*
七千円	**nana-sen-en**	*7,000 yen*

DIALOGUE

Study the dialogue below. Practice until you no longer need to refer to the Japanese half.

Store clerk : いらしゃいませ。
　　　　　　　Irasshaimase.
　　　　　　　Welcome!
Customer : あの青い花びんを見せて下さい。
　　　　　　　Ano aoi kabin o misete kudasai.
　　　　　　　Please show (me) that blue vase.

Store clerk : 青いのですか。どうぞ。

Aoi-no[1] desu ka? Dōzo.

The blue one? Please (have a look at it).

Customer : ちょっと大きいですね。

Chotto ōkii desu ne.

It's a little (too) big, isn't it?

もっと小さいのを見せて下さい。

Motto chiisai-no o misete kudasai.

Please show me a smaller one.

Store clerk : これはいかがですか。

Kore wa ikaga desu ka?

How about this one?

Customer : この花びんはいくらですか。

Kono kabin wa ikura desu ka?

How much is this vase?

Store clerk : 七千円です。

Nana-sen-en desu.

It's 7,000 yen.

Customer : これを下さい。

Kore o kudasai.

Please give me this one.

 POINTS TO REMEMBER

1. ADJECTIVE/NOUN + **no**: ADJECTIVE/NOUN one

   No is added to an adjective or a noun to make a modified pronoun.

   EXAMPLES: 青いのを見せて下さい。

   Aoi-no o misete kudasai.

   Please show me a blue one.

   茶色のを下さい。

   Chairo-no o kudasai.

   Please give me a brown one.

ADDITIONAL WORDS

Study these new words and clearly pronounce them aloud. Then proceed
to the exercises.

Currency (-en)

十円	**jū-en**	*10 yen*
五十円	**go-jū-en**	*50 yen*
百円	**hyaku-en**	*100 yen*
百五十円	**hyaku-go-jū-en**	*150 yen*
二百円	**ni-hyaku-en**	*200 yen*
三百円	**san-byaku-en**	*300 yen*
四百円	**yon-hyaku-en**	*400 yen*
五百円	**go-hyaku-en**	*500 yen*
六百円	**rop-pyaku-en**	*600 yen*
七百円	**nana-hyaku-en**	*700 yen*
八百円	**hap-pyaku-en**	*800 yen*
九百円	**kyū-hyaku-en**	*900 yen*
千円	**sen-en**	*1,000 yen*
千九百円	**sen-kyū-hyaku-en**	*1,900 yen*
二千円	**ni-sen-en**	*2,000 yen*
三千円	**san-zen-en**	*3,000 yen*
四千円	**yon-sen-en**	*4,000 yen*
五千円	**go-sen-en**	*5,000 yen*
六千円	**roku-sen-en**	*6,000 yen*
八千円	**has-sen-en**	*8,000 yen*
一万円	**ichi-man-en**	*10,000 yen*
絵	**e**	*painting*
人形	**ningyō**	*doll*
おもちゃ	**omocha**	*toy*
茶色	**chairo**	*brown*
赤い	**akai**	*red*
黒い	**kuroi**	*black*
白い	**shiroi**	*white*
高い	**takai**	*expensive*
安い	**yasui**	*inexpensive*

EXERCISES

A. Practice saying the following sentences in Japanese. Repeat the exercises until you no longer need to refer to the Japanese half.

1. *Please show me that vase.* — **Ano kabin o misete kudasai.** — あの花びんを見せて下さい。

   Please show me that doll. — **Ano ningyō o misete kudasai.** — あの人形を見せて下さい。

   Please show me that toy. — **Ano omocha o misete kudasai.** — あのおもちゃを見せて下さい。

   Please show me that painting. — **Ano e o misete kudasai.** — あの絵を見せて下さい。

2. *Please show me a small one.* — **Chiisai-no o misete kudasai.** — 小さいのを見せて下さい。

   Please show me a red one. — **Akai-no o misete kudasai.** — 赤いのを見せて下さい。

   Please show me a black one. — **Kuroi-no o misete kudasai.** — 黒いのを見せて下さい。

   Please show me a brown one. — **Chairo-no o misete kudasai.** — 茶色のを見せて下さい。

3. *Please show me a smaller one.* — **Motto chiisai-no o misete kudasai.** — もっと小さいのを見せて下さい。

   Please show me a bigger one. — **Motto ōkii-no o misete kudasai.** — もっと大きいのを見せて下さい。

   Please show me a less expensive one. — **Motto yasui-no o misete kudasai.** — もっと安いのを見せて下さい。

4. *This is a little (too) expensive.* — **Kore wa chotto takai desu.** — これはちょっと高いです。

   This is a little (too) small. — **Kore wa chotto chiisai desu.** — これはちょっと小さいです。

   This is a little (too) big. — **Kore wa chotto ōkii desu.** — これはちょっと大きいです。

5. *How much is this?* — **Kore wa ikura desu ka?** — これはいくらですか。

   How much is this blue vase? — **Kono aoi kabin wa ikura desu ka?** — この青い花びんはいくらですか。

   How much is the white one? — **Shiroi-no wa ikura desu ka?** — 白いのはいくらですか。

   How much is the big one? — **Ōkii-no wa ikura desu ka?** — 大きいのはいくらですか。

6. *It's 5,000 yen.*   **Go-sen-en desu**   五千円です。

    It's 7,000 yen.   **Nana-sen-en desu.**   七千円です。

    It's 1,800 yen.   **Sen-hap-pyaku-en desu.**   千八百円です。

    It's 950 yen.   **Kyū-hyaku-go-jū-en desu.**   九百五十円です。

    It's 10,000 yen.   **Ichi-man-en desu.**   一万円です。

7. *Please give me this blue vase.*   **Kono aoi kabin o kudasai.**   この青い花びんを下さい。

    Please give me the brown one.   **Chairo-no o kudasai.**   茶色のを下さい。

    Please give me the inexpensive one.   **Yasui-no o kudasai.**   安いのを下さい。

    Please give me that small one.   **Ano chiisai-no o kudasai.**   あの小さいのを下さい。

B. Ask the store clerk:

1. to show you that doll
2. to show you a big one
3. to show you a more expensive one
4. to tell you the price of this doll

ANSWERS

B.

1. **Ano ningyō o misete kudasai.** あの人形を見せて下さい。
2. **Ōkii-no o misete kudasai.** 大きいのを見せて下さい。
3. **Motto takai-no o misete kudasai.** もっと高いのを見せて下さい。
4. **Kono ningyō wa ikura desu ka?** この人形はいくらですか。

LESSON 15

What Did You Do Yesterday?

VOCABULARY

Study these words and clearly pronounce them aloud. Then proceed to the dialogue.

村田	**Murata**	*Murata* (a family name)
奈良	**Nara**	*Nara* (a city name)
大仏	**daibutsu**	*a large statue of Buddha*
見物	**kenbutsu**	*sightseeing*
観光バス	**kankō-basu**	*sightseeing bus*
車	**kuruma**	*car*
しました（する）	**shimashita[1] (suru)**	*did*
行きました（行く）	**ikimashita (iku)**	*went*
に	**ni[2, 3]**	*to (do); for (the purpose of)*
も	**mo[4]**	*also; too*
撮りました（撮る）	**torimashita (toru)**	*took (a picture)*
撮りませんでした。	**torimasen deshita[5]**	*did not take (a picture)*

DIALOGUE

Study the dialogue below. Practice until you no longer need to refer to the Japanese half.

Murata : きのうはいい天気でしたね。何をしましたか。
        Kinō wa ii tenki deshita ne. Nani o shimashita[1] ka?
        Yesterday was good weather, wasn't it? What did you do?
Wright : 友達と一緒に奈良へ行きました。
        Tomodachi to issho ni Nara e ikimashita.
        I went to Nara with my friend.
Murata : 何をしに行きましたか。
        Nani o shi ni[2] ikimashita ka?
        What did you go (there) for? (lit., go to do what?)

Wright : 見物に行きました。
Kenbutsu ni[3] **ikimashita.**
We went sightseeing.

Murata : 車で行きましたか。
Kuruma de ikimashita ka?
Did you go by car?

Wright : いいえ、観光バスで行きました。
Iie, kankō-basu de ikimashita.
No. We went by a sightseeing bus.

Murata : 写真を撮りましたか。
Shashin o torimashita ka?
Did you take pictures?

Wright : はい、たくさん撮りました。
Hai, takusan torimashita.
Yes, I took many.

Murata : 大仏の写真も撮りましたか。
Daibutsu no shashin mo[4] **torimashita ka?**
Did you also take pictures of the large statue of Buddha?

Wright : いいえ、撮りませんでした。
Iie, torimasen deshita.[5]
No, I didn't.

 POINTS TO REMEMBER

1. To make the past tense of a verb, change the verb ending *-masu* to *-mashita*.

> EXAMPLES: 私はお土産を買います。
> **Watashi wa o-miyage o kaimasu.**
> *I buy/will buy a souvenir.*
> 私はお土産を買いました。
> **Watashi wa o-miyage o kaimashita.**
> *I bought a souvenir.*

2. **V(-masu) + ni + MOTION VERB**: go/come/return to do
This expression, indicating purpose, is used only with motion verbs such as **ikimasu**, **kimasu** and **kaerimasu** [go, come, and return]. **Ni** is added to the verb from which the *-masu* ending has been dropped.

> EXAMPLE: 私は映画を見に行きます。
> **Watashi wa eiga o mi ni ikimasu.**
> *I'll go to see a movie.*

3. NOUN + **ni** + MOTION VERB: go/come/return for NOUN

   Ni is added to an "activity" noun such as sightseeing or lunch, and indicates purpose.

   EXAMPLES: 佐藤さんは昼ご飯に行きます。

   > **Satō-san wa hiru-gohan ni ikimasu.**
   > *Mr. Sato will go for lunch.*
   > 佐藤さんは見物に行きます。
   > **Satō-san wa kenbutsu ni ikimasu.**
   > *Mr. Sato will go sightseeing.*

4. NOUN + **mo**: NOUN also/too

   Mo refers to the immediately preceding word and gives the meaning "also" or "too." It replaces **o** (an object marker) and **wa** (a topic or subject marker).

   EXAMPLES: 本を買いました。花びんも買いました。

   > **Hon o kaimashita. Kabin mo kaimashita.**
   > *1 bought a book. I also bought a flower vase.*
   > 父も医者です。
   > **Chichi mo isha desu.**
   > *My father also is a doctor.*

5. To make the negative past tense, change the verb ending *-mashita* to *-masen deshita*.

   EXAMPLES: コーヒーを飲みました。

   > **Kōhii o nomimashita.**
   > *I drank coffee.*
   > コーヒーを飲みませんでした。
   > **Kōhii o nomimasen deshita.**
   > *1 did not drink coffee.*

ADDITIONAL WORDS

Study these new words and clearly pronounce them aloud. Then proceed to the exercises.

けさ	**kesa**	*this morning*
ゆうべ	**yūbe**	*last night*
おととい	**ototoi**	*the day before yesterday*
去年	**kyo-nen**	*last year*
年	**-nen**	(a suffix used for years)
果物	**kudamono**	*fruit*
お菓子	**o-kashi**	*sweets*
食事	**shokuji**	*meal; dinner*
経済	**keizai**	*economics*
歴史	**rekishi**	*history*
神社	**jinja**	*Shinto shrine*
公園	**kōen**	*park*
散歩	**sanpo**	*walk; stroll*

EXERCISES

A. Practice saying the following sentences in Japanese. Repeat the exercises until you no longer need to refer to the Japanese half.

1. *What did you do yesterday?*   **Kinō nani o shimashita ka?**   きのう何をしましたか。

   What did you see yesterday?   **Kinō nani o mimashita ka?**   きのう何を見ましたか。

   What did you buy yesterday?   **Kinō nani o kaimashita ka?**   きのう何を買いましたか。

   What did you drink yesterday?   **Kinō nani o nomimashita ka?**   きのう何を飲みましたか。

   What did you eat yesterday?   **Kinō nani o tabemashita ka?**   きのう何を食べましたか。

2. *I went to Kyoto to see Buddhist temples.* **Kyōto e o-tera o mi ni ikimashita.** 京都へお寺をに行きました。

I went to Kyoto to buy a history book. **Kyōto e rekishi no hon o kai ni ikimashita.** 京都へ歴史の本を買いに行きました。

I went to Kyoto for dinner. **Kyōto e shokuji ni ikimashita.** 京都へ食事に行きました。

I went to Kyoto for the exhibition. **Kyōto e tenran-kai ni ikimashita.** 京都へ展覧会に行きました。

I went to Kyoto for sightseeing. **Kyōto e kenbutsu ni ikimashita.** 京都へ見物に行きました。

3. *Last month I went to the park for a walk.* **Sen-getsu kōen e sanpo ni ikimashita.** 先月公園へ散歩に行きました。

The day before yesterday, I went to the park for a walk. **Ototoi, kōen e sanpo ni ikimashita.** おととい、公園へ散歩に行きました。

Last week, I went to the park for a walk. **Sen-shū, kōen e sanpo ni ikimashita.** 先週、公園へ散歩に行きました。

4. *I saw the Shinto shrine.* **Jinja o mimashita.** 神社を見ました。

I ate supper at a restaurant. **Resutoran de ban-gohan o tabemashita.** レストランで晩ご飯を食べました。

I bought a history book. **Rekishi no hon o kaimashita.** 歴史の本を買いました。

I drank coffee at a coffee shop. **Kissaten de kōhii o nomimashita.** 喫茶店でコーヒーを飲みました。

I did some shopping. **Kaimono o shimashita.** 買い物をしました。

I did some sightseeing. **Kenbutsu o shimashita.** 見物をしました。

5. *Last night I went to bed at 10:00.* **Yūbe jū-ji ni nemashita.** ゆうべ十時に寝ました。

Last week I went to Nara by a sightseeing bus. **Sen-shū kankō-basu de Nara e ikimashita.** 先週観光バスで奈良へ行きました。

This morning I got up at 6:00. **Kesa roku-ji ni okimashita.** けさ六時に起きました。

Last year I took some pictures. **Kyo-nen shashin o torimashita.** 去年写真を撮りました。

6. *I saw a temple.*   **O-tera o mimashita. Jinja** お寺を見ました。
   I also saw a shrine.   **mo mimashita.** 神社も見ました。
   I ate fruit. I also   **Kudamono o tabemashita.** 果物を食べまし
     ate sweets.   **O-kashi mo tabemashita.** た。お菓子も食
                                                   べました。

   I read a history   **Rekishi no hon o** 歴史の本を読み
     book. I also read   **yomimashita. Keizai no** ました。経済の
     an economics book.   **hon mo yomimashita.** 本も読みました。

7. *I took many pictures.*   **Shashin o takusan** 写真をたくさん撮
                                     torimashita. りました。
   I saw many temples.   **O-tera o takusan** お寺をたくさん見
                                     mimashita. ました。
   I bought many   **O-miyage o takusan** お土産をたくさん
     souvenirs.   **kaimashita.** 買いました。

8. *I didn't return at*   **Gogo san-ji ni kaerimasen** 午後三時に帰り
     3:00 P.M.   **deshita.** ませんでした。
   I didn't stay at a   **Hoteru ni tomarimasen** ホテルに泊まりま
     hotel.   **deshita.** せんでした。
   I didn't go by taxi.   **Takushii de ikimasen** タクシーで行きま
                                     deshita. せんでした。

B. Answer the following questions using the cue words.

1. **Kinō doko e ikimashita ka?**
きのうどこへ行きましたか。
(Nara) _____

2. **Kaimono o shimashita ka?**
買い物をしましたか。
Iie, _____

3. **Ototoi nani o shimashita ka?**
おととい何をしましたか。
(went to Kyoto to see temples) _____

4. **O-miyage o takusan kaimashita ka?**
お土産をたくさん買いましたか。
Hai, _____

5. **Yūbe nani o shimashita ka?**
   ゆうべ何をしましたか。
   (read an economics book) _____

6. **Itsu shokuji ni ikimashita ka?**
   いつ食事に行きましたか。
   (last week) _____

7. **Kissaten de kōhii o nomimashita ka?**
   喫茶店でコーヒーを飲みましたか。
   Iie, _____ . (black tea) _____ .

8. **O-kashi o tabemashita ka?**
   お菓子を食べましたか。
   Hai, _____

9. **Kudamono mo tabemashita ka?**
   果物も食べましたか。
   Hai, _____

   Iie, _____

ANSWERS

B.

1. **Nara e ikimashita.** 奈良へ行きました。
2. **Iie, shimasen deshita.** いいえ、しませんでした。
3. **Kyōto e o-tera o mi ni ikimashita.** 京都へお寺を見に行きました。
4. **Hai, takusan kaimashita.** はい、たくさん買いました。
5. **Keizai no hon o yomimashit.** 経済の本を読みました。
6. **Sen-shū ikimashita.** 先週行きました。
7. **Iie, nomimasen deshita. Kō-cha o nomimashita.** いいえ、飲みませんでした。紅茶を飲みました。
8. **Hai, tabemashita.** はい、食べました。
9. **Hai, kudamono mo tabemashita.** はい、果物も食べました。
   Iie, kudamono wa tabemasen deshita. いいえ、果物は食べませんでした。

LESSON 16

Can You Cook Sukiyaki?

VOCABULARY

Study these words and clearly pronounce them aloud. Then proceed to the dialogue.

福田	**Fukuda**	(a family name)
料理	**ryōri**	*cooking*
すきやき	**sukiyaki**	*a popular Japanese dish*
お寿司	**o-sushi**	*vinegared rice and raw fish*
作る	**tsukuru**	*to make*
できます（できる）	**dekimasu**[1] **(dekiru)**	*can; is able to; is possible*
できません	**dekimasen**	*cannot; is not able to; is not possible*
上手	**jōzu**	*good; skillful*
でも	**demo**	*but*

DIALOGUE

Study the dialogue below. Practice until you no longer need to refer to the Japanese half.

Fukuda : あなたは料理ができますか。
      Anata wa ryōri ga dekimasu[1] **ka?**
      Can you cook? (lit., As for you, is cooking possible?)
Olson : はい、できます。
      Hai, dekimasu.
      Yes, I can.
Fukuda : すきやきを作る事ができますか。
      Sukiyaki o tsukuru-koto[2] **ga dekimasu ka?**
      Can you make sukiyaki? (lit., Is making sukiyaki possible?)
Olson : いいえ、できません。レストランで食べます。
      Iie, dekimasen. Resutoran de tabemasu.
      No, I can't. I eat it at restaurants.

Fukuda : お寿司を作る事は？
O-sushi o tsukuru-koto wa?
How about making sushi?

Olson : できます。先週学校で作りました。でも、上手ではありません。
Dekimasu. Sen-shū gakkō de tsukurimashita. Demo, jōzu dewa arimasen.
I can. We made it at school last week. But, I am not good at it.

 POINTS TO REMEMBER

1. (NOUN + **wa**) + [SOMETHING] + **ga dekimasu**: NOUN can do [SOMETHING]
   Can do is replaceable with *can play, speak, make,* etc.
   EXAMPLE: カーターさんは日本語ができます。
   Kātā-san wa Nihon-go ga dekimasu.
   Mr. Carter can speak Japanese.
   (*lit.*, As for Mr. Carter, Japanese is possible.)
   Note that **wa** (a topic marker) and **ga** (a subject marker) can be used in the same sentence.

2. (NOUN + **wa**) + [VERB + **koto**] + **ga dekimasu**: NOUN can do [GERUND].
   Koto is used to make a gerund out of a verb.
   EXAMPLE: 天ぷらを作る事ができます。
   Tenpura o tsukuru-koto ga dekimasu.
   I can make tenpura.
   (*lit.*, As for me, making tenpura is possible.)

ADDITIONAL WORDS

Study these new words and clearly pronounce them aloud. Then proceed to the exercises.

話す	**hanasu**	*to speak*
泳ぐ	**oyogu**	*to swim*
歌う	**utau**	*to sing*
教える	**oshieru**	*to teach*
来る	**kuru**	*to come*
英語	**Ei-go**	*English language*
語	**-go**	(a suffix used for languages)
ドイツ語	**Doitsu-go**	*German language*
フランス語	**Furansu-go**	*French language*
日本語	**Nihon-go/Nippon-go**	*Japanese language*

ゴルフ	**gorufu**	*golf*
テニス	**tenisu**	*tennis*
歌	**uta**	*song*
へた	**heta**	*poor; unskillful*

EXERCISES

A. Practice saying the following sentences in Japanese. Repeat the exercises until you no longer need to refer to the Japanese half.

1. *Can you cook?*   **Anata wa ryōri ga dekimasu ka?**   あなたは料理ができますか。

 Can you play golf?   **Anata wa gorufu ga dekimasu ka?**   あなたはゴルフができますか。

 Can you play tennis?   **Anata wa tenisu ga dekimasu ka?**   あなたはテニスができますか。

 Can you speak English?   **Anata wa Ei-go ga dekimasu ka?**   あなたは英語ができますか。

2. *Can you make sushi?*   **O-sushi o tsukuru-koto ga dekimasu ka?**   お寿司を作る事ができますか。

 Can you teach English?   **Ei-go o oshieru-koto ga dekimasu ka?**   英語を教える事ができますか。

 Can you come tomorrow?   **Ashita kuru-koto ga dekimasu ka?**   明日来る事ができますか。

 Can you play golf?   **Gorufu o suru-koto ga dekimasu ka?**   ゴルフをする事ができますか。

3. *I can't play the piano.*   **Watashi wa piano ga dekimasen.**   私はピアノができません。

 I can't speak French.   **Watashi wa Furansu-go ga dekimasen.**   私はフランス語ができません。

 I can't play tennis.   **Watashi wa tenisu ga dekimasen.**   私はテニスができません。

 I can't sing songs.   **Watashi wa uta ga dekimasen.**   私は歌ができません。

4. *I can't swim.*	**Oyogu-koto ga dekimasen.**	泳ぐ事ができません。
I can't sing songs.	**Uta o utau-koto ga dekimasen.**	歌を歌う事ができません。
I can't teach Japanese.	**Nihon-go o oshieru-koto ga dekimasen.**	日本語を教える事ができません。
5. *Miss Sato is good/ poor at golf.*	**Satō-san wa gorufu ga jōzu/heta desu.**	佐藤さんはゴルフが上手／へたです。
Miss Sato is good/ poor at cooking.	**Satō-san wa ryōri ga jōzu/heta desu.**	佐藤さんは料理が上手／へたです。
Miss Sato is good/ poor at German.	**Satō-san wa Doitsu-go ga jōzu/heta desu.**	佐藤さんはドイツ語が上手／へたです。
6. *I am not good at making sukiyaki.*	**Watashi wa sukiyaki o tsukuru-koto ga jōzu dewa arimasen.**	私はすきやきを作る事が上手ではありません。
I am not good at speaking Japanese.	**Watashi wa Nihon-go o hanasu-koto ga jōzu dewa arimasen.**	私は日本語を話す事が上手ではありません。
I am not good at teaching songs.	**Watashi wa uta o oshieru-koto ga jōzu dewa arimasen.**	私は歌を教える事が上手ではありません。

B. Answer the following questions using the cue words.

1. **Anata wa ryōri ga dekimasu ka?**
   あなたは料理ができますか
   Hai, _____

2. **Anata wa Doitsu-go ga dekimasu ka?**
   あなたはドイツ語ができますか
   Iie, _____

3. **Piano ga dekimasu ka?**
   ピアノができますか
   Hai, _____ . (not good) **Demo,** _____ .

4. **Ei-go o oshieru-koto ga dekimasu ka?**
   英語を教える事ができますか
   Hai, _____

5. **Sukiyaki o tsukuru-koto ga dekimasu ka?**
   すきやきを作る事ができますか
   Iie, _____

6. **Tenisu ga dekimasu ka?**
   テニスができますか
   Hai, _____ . (poor) **Demo,** _____ .

ANSWERS

B.
1. **Hai, dekimasu.** はい、できます。
2. **Iie, dekimasen.** いいえ、できません。
3. **Hai, dekimasu. Demo, jōzu dewa arimasen.** はい、できます。でも、上手 ではありません。
4. **Hai, dekimasu.** はい、できます。
5. **Iie, dekimasen.** いいえ、できません。
6. **Hai, dekimasu. Demo, heta desu.** はい、できます。でも、へたです。

LESSON 17

Do You Like to Travel?

VOCABULARY

Study these words and clearly pronounce them aloud. Then proceed to
the dialogue.

中野	**Nakano**	(a family name)
手紙	**tegami**	*letter*
好き	**suki**[1]	*like; be fond of*
書きました（書く）	**kakimashita (kaku)**	*wrote (to write)*
と	**to**	*and* (used to connect two nouns)
に	**ni**[3]	*to* (an indirect object marker)

DIALOGUE

Study the dialogue below. Practice until you no longer need to refer to the
Japanese half.

Nakano : あなたは旅行が好きですか。
　　　　Anata wa ryokō ga suki[1] **desu ka?**
　　　　Do you like to travel?

Green : はい、好きです。先週、京都と奈良へ行きました。
　　　　Hai, suki desu. Sen-shū, Kyōto to Nara e ikimashita.
　　　　Yes, I do. Last week I went to Kyoto and Nara.

Nakano : 写真を撮るのが好きですか。
　　　　Shashin o toru-no[2] **ga suki desu ka?**
　　　　Do you like taking pictures?

Green : はい、好きです。
　　　　Hai, suki desu.
　　　　Yes, I do.

Nakano : アメリカの友達に手紙を書きましたか。

Amerika no tomodachi ni[3] tegami o kakimashita ka?

Did you write letters to (your) friends in America?

Green : いいえ、手紙を書くのは好きではありません。

Iie, tegami o kaku-no wa[4] suki dewa arimasen.

No, I don't like writing letters.

📖 POINTS TO REMEMBER

1. (NOUN + **wa**) + [SOMETHING] + **ga suki desu**: NOUN like [SOMETHING]
   EXAMPLE: 母は花が好きです。
   Haha wa hana ga suki desu.
   My mother likes flowers.

2. (NOUN + **wa**) + [VERB + **no**] + **ga suki desu**: NOUN like [GERUND]
   No is used to make a gerund out of a verb.
   EXAMPLE: 福田さんは泳ぐのが好きです。
   Fukuda-san wa oyogu-no ga suki desu.
   Mr. Fukuda likes swimming.
   Instead of [VERB + **no**], [VERB + **koto**] can also be used.
   EXAMPLE: 父は手紙を書くの/書く事が好きです。
   Chichi wa tegami o kaku-no/kaku-koto ga suki desu.
   My father likes writing letters.

3. NOUN + **ni**: to NOUN
   When added to an indirect object of a verb, **ni** becomes an indirect object marker.
   EXAMPLE: 父に手紙を書きました。
   Chichi ni tegami o kakimashita.
   I wrote a letter to my father.

4. The particle **ga** changes to **wa** in negative sentences (*see* Lesson 10).

ADDITIONAL WORDS

Study these new words and clearly pronounce them aloud. Then proceed to the exercises.

集める	**atsumeru**	*to collect*
切手	**kitte**	*stamp*
動物	**dōbutsu**	*animal*
鳥	**tori**	*bird*
海	**umi**	*sea*
山	**yama**	*mountain*
山のぼり	**yama-nobori**	*mountain climbing*
音楽	**ongaku**	*music*
秋	**aki**	*autumn*
冬	**fuyu**	*winter*
春	**haru**	*spring*
夏	**natsu**	*summer*

EXERCISES

A. Practice saying the following sentences in Japanese. Repeat the exercises until you no longer need to refer to the Japanese half.

1. *Do you like to travel?* **Anata wa ryokō ga suki desu ka?** あなたは旅行が好きですか。

   Do you like music? **Anata wa ongaku ga suki desu ka?** あなたは音楽が好きですか。

   Do you like animals? **Anata wa dōbutsu ga suki desu ka?** あなたは動物が好きですか。

   Do you like mountain climbing? **Anata wa yama-nobori ga suki desu ka?** あなたは山のぼりが好きですか。

2. *Do you like taking pictures?* **Shashin o toru-no ga suki desu ka?** 写真を撮るのが好きですか。

   Do you like swimming? **Oyogu-no ga suki desu ka?** 泳ぐのが好きですか。

   Do you like writing letters? **Tegami o kaku-no ga suki desu ka?** 手紙を書くのが好きですか。

   Do you like singing songs? **Uta o utau-no ga suki desu ka?** 歌を歌うのが好きですか。

3. *I like birds.*   **Watashi wa tori ga suki desu.**   私は鳥が好きです。

   I like mountains.   **Watashi wa yama ga suki desu.**   私は山が好きです。

   I like spring and autumn.   **Watashi wa haru to aki ga suki desu.**   私は春と秋が好きです。

4. *I like collecting stamps.*   **Kitte o atsumeru-no ga suki desu.**   切手を集めるのが好きです。

   I like teaching tennis.   **Tenisu o oshieru-no ga suki desu.**   テニスを教えるのが好きです。

   I like swimming in the sea.   **Umi de oyogu-no ga suki desu.**   海で泳ぐのが好きです。

5. *I don't like animals.*   **Watashi wa dōbutsu wa suki dewa arimasen.**   私は動物は好きではありません。

   I don't like the sea.   **Watashi wa umi wa suki dewa arimasen.**   私は海は好きではありません。

   I don't like summer and winter.   **Watashi wa natsu to fuyu wa suki dewa arimasen.**   私は夏と冬は好きではありません。

6. *I don't like staying at hotels.*   **Hoteru ni tomaru-no wa suki dewa arimasen.**   ホテルに泊まるのは好きではありません。

   I don't like coming here.   **Koko e kuru-no wa suki dewa arimasen.**   ここへ来るのは好きではありません。

   I don't like reading books.   **Hon o yomu-no wa suki dewa arimasen.**   本を読むのは好きではありません。

B. Answer the following questions using the cue words.

1. **Anata wa umi ga suki desu ka?**
あなたは海が好きですか。
Hai, ————————————————————————

2. **Tori ga suki desu ka?**
鳥が好きですか。
Iie, ————————————————————————

3. **Kitte o atsumeru-no ga suki desu ka?**
   切手を集めるのが好きですか。
   Hai, _____

4. **Tenisu o oshieru-no ga suki desu ka?**
   テニスを教えるのが好きですか。
   Iie, _____

C. Tell that you like the following:
1. trips
2. music
3. spring and autumn
4. swimming in the sea
5. speaking Japanese

D. Tell that you don't like the following:
1. mountain climbing
2. animals
3. summer and winter
4. singing songs
5. writing letters

ANSWERS

B.
1. **Hai, umi ga suki desu.** はい、海が好きです。
2. **Iie, tori wa suki dewa arimasen.** いいえ、鳥は好きではありません。
3. **Hai, kitte o atsumeru-no ga suki desu.** はい、切手を集めるのが好きです。
4. **Iie, tenisu o oshieru-no wa suki dewa arimasen.**
   いいえ、テニスを教えるのは好きではありません。

C.
1. **Ryokō ga suki desu.** 旅行が好きです。
2. **Ongaku ga suki desu.** 音楽が好きです。
3. **Haru to aki ga suki desu.** 春と秋が好きです。
4. **Umi de oyogu-no ga suki desu.** 海で泳ぐのが好きです。
5. **Nihon-go o hanasu-no ga suki desu.** 日本語を話すのが好きです。

D.
1. **Yama-nobori wa suki dewa arimasen.** 山のぼりは好きではありません。
2. **Dōbutsu wa suki dewa arimasen.** 動物は好きではありません。
3. **Natsu to fuyu wa suki dewa arimasen.** 夏と冬は好きではありません。
4. **Uta o utau-no wa suki dewa arimasen.** 歌を歌うのは好きではありません。
5. **Tegami o kaku-no wa suki dewa arimasen.** 手紙を書くのは好きではありません。

Where Do You Want to Go?

VOCABULARY

Study these words and clearly pronounce them aloud. Then proceed to the dialogue.

安田	**Yasuda**	(a family name)
熱海	**Atami**	(famous hot spring resort)
温泉	**onsen**	*hot spring*
旅館	**ryokan**	*inn*
週末	**shū-matsu**	*weekend*
末	**-matsu**	*the end of ~*
便利	**benri**	*convenient*
行きたい	**iki-tai**[1]	*want to go*
たい	**-tai**	(a suffix meaning "want to")
そして	**soshite**	*and; and then; also*
どう	**dō**	*how*
方	**hō**[2]	*side* (used for comparison)

DIALOGUE

Study the dialogue below. Practice until you no longer need to refer to the Japanese half.

Yasuda : あなたは週末にどこへ行きたいですか。
Anata wa shū-matsu ni doko e iki-tai[1] **desu ka?**
Where do you want to go on the weekend?

Cooper : 温泉へ行きたいです。そして、日本の旅館に泊まりたいです。
Onsen e iki-tai desu. Soshite, Nihon no ryokan ni tomari-tai desu.
I want to go to a hot spring. And, I want to stay at a Japanese inn.

Yasuda : 熱海はどうですか。東京から近いです。
Atami wa dō desu ka? Tōkyō kara chikai desu.
How about Atami? It's near (from) Tokyo.

Cooper : 車で行く事ができますか。
Kuruma de iku-koto ga dekimasu ka?
Can I go by car?

Yasuda : はい、できます。でも電車の方が便利です。
Hai, dekimasu. Demo densha no hō[2] ga benri desu.
Yes, you can. But a train is more convenient.

 POINTS TO REMEMBER

1. (NOUN + **wa**) + **V-tai desu**: NOUN want to do
   For all verbs, to make the **V-tai** form, drop the **-masu** ending and add **-tai**.

   EXAMPLES: 買います **kaimasu** + たい **tai**
   → 買いたい **kaitai** (*want to buy*)
   します **shimasu** + たい **tai**
   → したい **shitai** (*want to do*)

   EXAMPLES: 車を買いたいです。
   Kuruma o kai-tai desu.
   I want to buy a car.

   刺身を食べたいです。
   Sashimi o tabe-tai desu.
   I want to eat sashimi.

   ゴルフをしたいです。
   Gorufu o shi-tai desu.
   I want to play golf.

2. (NOUN + **no** + **hō**) + **ga** + (ADJECTIVE) **desu**: NOUN is more (ADJECTIVE)
   This is used when comparing two things.

   EXAMPLE: 飛行機のほうが早いです。
   Hikō-ki no hō ga hayai desu.
   An airplane is faster.

ADDITIONAL WORDS

Study these new words and clearly pronounce them aloud. Then proceed to the exercises.

帽子	**bōshi**	*hat; cap*
靴	**kutsu**	*shoes*
セーター	**sētā**	*sweater*
履く	**haku**	*to wear (shoes)*
かぶる	**kaburu**	*to wear (a hat)*
着る	**kiru**	*to wear (a sweater)*
弾く	**hiku**	*to play (the piano)*
速い	**hayai**	*fast*
遅い	**osoi**	*slow*
きれい	**kirei**	*pretty*
楽	**raku**	*comfortable*
静か	**shizuka**	*quiet*

EXERCISES

A. Practice saying the following sentences in Japanese. Repeat the exercises until you no longer need to refer to the Japanese half.

1. *What do you want to do?* **Anata wa nani o shi-tai desu ka?** あなたは何をしたいですか。

   What do you want to buy? **Anata wa nani o kai-tai desu ka?** あなたは何を買いたいですか。

   What do you want to read? **Anata wa nani o yomi-tai desu ka?** あなたは何を読みたいですか。

   What do you want to drink? **Anata wa nani o nomi-tai desu ka?** あなたは何を飲みたいですか。

   What do you want to see? **Anata wa nani o mi-tai desu ka?** あなたは何を見たいですか。

2. *Where do you want to go?* **Doko e iki-tai desu ka?** どこへ行きたいですか。

   Where do you want to eat? **Doko de tabe-tai desu ka?** どこで食べたいですか。

   Where do you want to stay? **Doko ni tomari-tai desu ka?** どこに泊まりたいですか。

3. *I want to play golf.* **Gorufu o shi-tai desu.** ゴルフをしたいです。

I want to play the piano. **Piano o hiki-tai desu.** ピアノを弾きたいです。

I want to wear a sweater. **Sētā o ki-tai desu.** セーターを着たいです。

I want to wear white shoes. **Shiroi kutsu o haki-tai desu.** 白い靴を履きたいです。

I want to wear a blue hat. **Aoi bōshi o kaburi-tai desu.** 青い帽子をかぶりたいです。

4. *A train is more convenient.* **Densha no hō ga benri desu.** 電車の方が便利です。

An airplane is faster. **Hikō-ki no hō ga hayai desu.** 飛行機の方が速いです。

A ship is slower. **Fune no hō ga osoi desu.** 船の方が遅いです。

This flower is prettier. **Kono hana no hō ga kirei desu.** この花の方がきれいです。

This room is quieter. **Kono heya no hō ga shizuka desu.** この部屋の方が静かです。

This chair is more comfortable. **Kono isu no hō ga raku desu.** この椅子の方が楽です。

B. Answer the following questions using the cue words.

1. **Ashita doko e iki-tai desu ka?**
   あしたどこへ行きたいですか。
   (park) _____

2. **Shū-matsu ni nani o shi-tai desu ka?**
   週末に何をしたいですか。
   (go for shopping) _____

3. **Doko ni tomari-tai desu ka?**
   どこに泊まりたいですか。
   (Japanese inn) _____

4. **Resutoran de nani o tabe-tai desu ka?**
   レストランで何を食べたいですか。
   (sashimi and tenpura) _____

5. **Itsu onsen e iki-tai desu ka?**
いつ温泉へ行きたいですか。
(Saturday of next week) _____

6. **Doko de shashin o tori-tai desu ka?**
どこで写真を撮りたいですか。
(Atami) _____

7. **Densha de ikimasu ka?**
電車で行きますか。
(more convenient) **Hai. Densha no hō ga** _____

8. **Hikō-ki de iki-tai desu ka?**
飛行機で行きたいですか。
(faster) **Hai.** _____

9. **Fune de iki-tai desu ka?**
船で行きたいですか。
(more comfortable) **Hai.** _____

10. **Kono heya de hon o yomi-tai desu ka?**
この部屋で本を読みたいですか。
(quieter) **Hai.** _____

ANSWERS

B.
1. **Kōen e iki-tai desu.** 公園へ行きたいです。
2. **Kaimono ni iki-tai desu.** 買い物に行きたいです。
3. **Nihon no ryokan ni tomari-tai desu.** 日本の旅館に泊まりたいです。
4. **Sashimi to tenpura o tabe-tai desu.** 刺身と天ぷらを食べたいです。
5. **Rai-shū no Do-yōbi ni iki-tai desu.** 来週の土曜日に行きたいです。
6. **Atami de tori-tai desu.** 熱海で撮りたいです。
7. **Hai. (Densha no hō ga) benri desu.** はい、(電車の方が)便利です。
8. **Hai. Hikō-ki no hō ga hayai desu.** はい、飛行機の方が速いです。
9. **Hai. Fune no hō ga raku desu.** はい、船の方が楽です。
10. **Hai. Kono heya no hō ga shizuka desu.** はい、この部屋の方が静かです。

Which Button Is It?

VOCABULARY

Study these words and clearly pronounce them aloud. Then proceed to the dialogue.

切符	**kippu**	*ticket*
自動販売機	**jidō-hanbai-ki**	*vending machine*
機	**-ki**	(a suffix used for machines)
運賃表	**unchin-hyō**	*fare table*
表	**hyō**	*table; schedule*
ボタン	**botan**	*button*
お金	**o-kane**	*money*
どれ	**dore***	*which (one)*
どの	**dono***	*which*
まず	**mazu**	*first; to begin with*
入れる	**ireru**	*to put in*
押す	**osu**	*to push*

* The pronoun **dore** becomes **dono** when it modifies a following noun.

DIALOGUE

Study the dialogue below. Practice until you no longer need to refer to the Japanese half.

Tourist : 大阪行きの切符を下さい。
Ōsaka-yuki no kippu o kudasai.
Please give me a ticket for Osaka.

Clerk : 自動販売機で買って下さい。
Jidō-hanbai-ki de katte kudasai.[1]
Please buy it at a vending machine.

* * * * * *

Tourist : あれは何ですか。
Are wa nan desu ka?
What is that?

Yasuda : 運賃表です。
Unchin-hyō desu.
It's a fare table.

Tourist : 大阪はどれですか。
Ōsaka wa dore desu ka?
Which one is Osaka's?

Yasuda : あれです。五百十円です。
Are desu. Go-hyaku-jū-en desu.
That one. It's 510 yen.

Tourist : どのボタンですか。
Dono botan desu ka?
Which button is it?

Yasuda : まず、ここにお金を入れて下さい。それから、このボタンを押して下さい。
Mazu, koko ni o-kane o irete kudasai. Sore-kara, kono botan o oshite kudasai.
First, please put in money here. Then, please push this button.

📖 POINTS TO REMEMBER

1. **V-te kudasai**: Please do ~ (*lit.*, Please give your ~ing.)
   The **-te** form of the verb is equivalent to the English "~ing." How to make the **V-te** forms is explained on page 105.
   EXAMPLES: 英語を話して下さい。
   Ei-go de hanashite kudasai.
   Please speak in English.
   写真を撮って下さい。
   Shashin o totte kudasai.
   Please take a picture.

2. NOUN + **ni hairimasu**: enter NOUN
   Ni as used here indicates the place where a person moves into.
   EXAMPLE: 部屋に入りました。
   Heya ni hairimashita.
   I entered the room.

ADDITIONAL WORDS

Study these new words and clearly pronounce them aloud. Then proceed
to the exercises.

英語で	**Ei-go de**	*in English* (*see* Lesson 5, page 32)
大学	**daigaku**	*college; university*
辞書	**jisho**	*dictionary*
道	**michi**	*road; street*
店	**mise**	*store; shop*
家	**uchi**	*house; home*
片道	**katamichi**	*one-way*
往復	**ōfuku**	*round-trip*
もう一度	**mō ichido**	*once more*
もっとゆっくり	**motto yukkuri**	*slower*
言う	**iu**	*to say*
待つ	**matsu**	*to wait*
立つ	**tatsu**	*to stand*
急ぐ	**isogu**	*to hurry*
呼ぶ	**yobu**	*to call*
死ぬ	**shinu**	*to die*
入る	**hairu**	*to enter*
に入ります	**ni hairimasu**[2]	*enter* (*a room*)

THE V-TE FORM

The **V-te** forms of verbs are formed as follows:

Regular Verbs (GROUP 1)

1. Change the *-ku* endings to *-ite*.*
    EXAMPLE: 書く ka*ku* → 書いて ka*ite* (*write*)

2. Change the *-gu* endings to *-ide*.
    EXAMPLE: 急ぐ iso*gu* → 急いで iso*ide* (*hurry*)

3. Change the *-su* endings to *-shite*.
    EXAMPLES: 話す hana*su* → 話して hana*shite* (*speak*)
    　　　　　　押す o*su* → 押して o*shite* (*push*)

4. Change the *-bu*, *-mu*, and *-nu* endings to *-nde*.
    EXAMPLES: 呼ぶ yo*bu* → 呼んで yo*nde* (*call*)
    　　　　　　飲む no*mu* → 飲んで no*nde* (*drink*)
    　　　　　　読む yo*mu* → 読んで yo*nde* (*read*)
    　　　　　　死ぬ shi*nu* → 死んで shi*nde* (*die*)

5. Change the *-ru*, *-tsu*, and *-(w)u* endings to *-tte*.

> EXAMPLES: 帰る **kae*ru*** → 帰って **kae*tte*** (*return*)
> 入る **hai*ru*** → 入って **hai*tte*** (*enter*)
> 待つ **ma*tsu*** → 待って **ma*tte*** (*wait*)
> 立つ **ta*tsu*** → 立って **ta*tte*** (*stand*)
> 言う **i*u*** → 言って **i*tte*** (*say*)
> 買う **ka*u*** → 買って **ka*tte*** (*buy*)
> 行く **i*ku****** → 行って **i*tte*** (*go*)

* **Iku** is an exception. Note that the **-te** form is **itte**, not **iite**.

Semi-Regular Verbs (GROUP 2)
Change the *-ru* endings to *-te*.

> EXAMPLES: 食べる **tabe*ru*** → 食べて **tabe*te*** (*eat*)
> 見て **mi*ru*** → 見て **mi*te*** (*see*)

Irregular Verbs (GROUP 3)

> 来る **kuru** → 来て **kite** (*come*)
> する **suru** → して **shite** (*do*)

EXERCISES

A. Practice saying the following sentences in Japanese. Repeat the exercises until you no longer need to refer to the Japanese half.

1. *Please give me a ticket for Osaka.* **Ōsaka-yuki no kippu o kudasai.** 大阪行きの切符を下さい。

   Please give me a round-trip ticket. **Ōfuku (-kippu) o kudasai.** 往復（切符）を下さい。

   Please give me a one-way ticket. **Katamichi (-kippu) o kudasai.** 片道（切符）を下さい。

2. *Please write a letter.* **Tegami o kaite kudasai.** 手紙を書いて下さい。

   Please hurry. **Isoide kudasai.** 急いで下さい。

   Please push the button. **Botan o oshite kudasai.** ボタンを押して下さい。

   Please call a doctor. **Isha o yonde kudasai.** 医者を呼んで下さい。

   Please drink beer. **Biiru o nonde kudasai.** ビールを飲んで下さい。

   Please read this magazine. **Kono zasshi o yonde kudasai.** この雑誌を読んで下さい。

   Please return home. **Uchi e kaette kudasai.** 家へ帰って下さい。

Please enter the room.	**Heya ni haitte kudasai.**	部屋に入って下さい。
Please wait a little.	**Chotto matte kudasai.**	ちょっと待って下さい。
Please stand.	**Tatte kudasai.**	立って下さい。
Please say it once more.	**Mō ichido itte kudasai.**	もう一度言って下さい。
Please buy a souvenir.	**O-miyage o katte kudasai.**	お土産を買って下さい。
Please go to the post office.	**Yūbin-kyoku e itte kudasai.**	郵便局へ行って下さい。
Please eat lunch.	**Hiru-gohan o tabete kudasai.**	昼ご飯を食べて下さい。
Please look at the photo.	**Shashin o mite kudasai.**	写真を見て下さい。
Please come tomorrow.	**Ashita kite kudasai.**	あした来て下さい。
Please do some sightseeing.	**Kenbutsu o shite kudasai.**	見物をして下さい。
Please speak in English.	**Ei-go de hanashite kudasai.**	英語で話して下さい。
Please speak slower.	**Motto yukkuri hanashite kudasai.**	もっとゆっくり話して下さい。

3.
Which button is it?	**Dono botan desu ka?**	どのボタンですか。
Which college is it?	**Dono daigaku desu ka?**	どの大学ですか。
Which street is it?	**Dono michi desu ka?**	どの道ですか。
Which store is it?	**Dono mise desu ka?**	どの店ですか。

B. Fill in the blanks.

1. **Ōsaka-yuki no _____ o kudasai**. (ticket)
2. _____ **o** _____ . (round-trip ticket, please give me)
3. **Are wa** _____ **desu ka?** (what)
4. _____ **desu.** (fare table)
5. **Kono botan o** _____ . (please push)
6. **Jidō-hanbai-ki de** _____ . (please buy)
7. **Koko de** _____ . (please eat)
8. **Kono hon o** _____ . (please read)
9. **Ei-go de** _____ . (please speak)
10. **Kaimono o** _____ . (please do)
11. **Dono** _____ **desu ka?** (street)
12. **Dono** _____ **desu ka?** (dictionary)

C. Say the following sentences in Japanese.

1. Please put in money here.
2. Please go to the airport.
3. Please come at 1:30 P.M.
4. Please speak slower.
5. Please buy a one-way ticket.
6. Please say it once more.
7. Please wait a little.
8. Please enter the conference room.
9. Which house is it?
10. Which train is it?
11. Which college is it?
12. Which vending machine is it?

ANSWERS

B.
1. **kippu** 切符
2. **Ōfuku o kudasai.** 往復を下さい。
3. **nan** 何
4. **Unchin-hyō** 運賃表
5. **oshite kudasai.** 押して下さい。
6. **katte kudasai.** 買って下さい。
7. **tabete kudasai.** 食べて下さい。
8. **yonde kudasai.** 読んで下さい。
9. **hanashite kudasai.** 話して下さい。
10. **shite kudasai.** して下さい。
11. **michi** 道
12. **jisho** 辞書

C.
1. **Koko ni o-kane o irete kudasai.** ここにお金を入れて下さい。
2. **Kūkō e itte kudasai.** 空港へ行って下さい。
3. **Gogo ichi-ji-han ni kite kudasai.** 午後一時半に来て下さい。
4. **Motto yukkuri hanashite kudasai.** もっとゆっくり話して下さい。
5. **Katamichi o katte kudasai.** 片道を買って下さい。
6. **Mō ichido itte kudasai.** もう一度言って下さい。
7. **Chotto matte kudasai.** ちょっと待って下さい。
8. **Kaigi-shitsu ni haitte kudasai.** 会議室に入って下さい。
9. **Dono uchi desu ka?** どの家ですか。
10. **Dono densha desu ka?** どの電車ですか。
11. **Dono daigaku desu ka?** どの大学ですか。
12. **Dono jidō-hanbai-ki desu ka?** どの自動販売機ですか。

Shall We Go Together?

VOCABULARY

Study these words and clearly pronounce them aloud. Then proceed to the dialogue.

和田	**Wada**	(a family name)
ヒルさん	**Hiru-san**	*Mr./Mrs./Miss Hill*
今晩	**kon-ban**	*tonight; this evening*
もしもし	**Moshi-moshi.**	*Hello. (on the telephone)*
じゃあ、また（また）	**Jā, mata. (mata)**	*See you later/again. (again)*
しばらく	**shibaraku**	*for a while; for a long time*
暇	**hima**	*free (not busy)*
忙しい	**isogashii**	*busy*
すばらしい	**subarashii**	*wonderful*
行きましょうか（行く）	**ikimashō ka?**[1] **(iku)**	*shall I/we go? (to go)*
会いましょう（会う）	**aimashō**[2] **(au)**	*let's meet (to meet)*
〜頃	**~ goro**	*about ~ (approximate point in time)*

DIALOGUE

Study the dialogue below. Practice until you no longer need to refer to the Japanese half.

Wada : もしもし、ヒルさんですか。和田です。
      Moshi-moshi, Hiru-san desu ka? Wada desu.
      Hello, Mr. Hill? This is Wada.

Hill : しばらくですね。お元気ですか。
      Shibaraku desu ne. O-genki desu ka?
      It's been a long time (since we met), hasn't it? How are you?

Wada : はい。ありがとう、元気です。今晩忙しいですか。
      Hai, arigatō, genki desu. Kon-ban isogashii desu ka?
      Yes, I'm fine, thanks. Are you busy this evening?

Hill　：いいえ、暇です。
　　　　Iie, hima desu.
　　　　No. I'm free.

Wada　：歌舞伎の切符があります。一緒に行きましょうか。
　　　　Kabuki no kippu ga arimasu. Issho ni ikimashō ka?[1]
　　　　I have tickets for Kabuki. Shall we go together?

Hill　：すばらしいですね。行きたいです。
　　　　Subarashii desu ne! Iki-tai desu.
　　　　That's wonderful! I'd like to go.

Wada　：四時頃歌舞伎座の前で会いましょう。
　　　　Yo-ji goro Kabuki-za no mae de aimashō.[2]
　　　　Let's meet in front of the Kabuki Theater about 4:00.

Hill　：はい。じゃあ、また。
　　　　Hai. Jā, mata.
　　　　Yes. See you later.

POINTS TO REMEMBER

1. **V-mashō ka?** Shall I/we do?
   To make the **V-mashō** forms, change *-masu* to *-mashō*.
   > EXAMPLE: 一緒にテレビを見ましょうか。
   > > **Issho ni terebi o mimashō ka?**
   > > *Shall we watch TV together?*

2. **V-mashō**: let's do ~
   > EXAMPLE: 駅で会いましょう。
   > > **Eki de aimashō.**
   > > *Let's meet at the station.*

ADDITIONAL WORDS

Study these new words and clearly pronounce them aloud. Then proceed to the exercises.

あげる	**ageru**	*to give*
開ける	**akeru**	*to open*
点ける	**tsukeru**	*to turn on* (*the light*)
消す	**kesu**	*to turn off* (*the light*)
休む	**yasumu**	*to rest*
招待する	**shōtai suru***	*to invite*
招待	**shōtai**	*invitation*
電灯	**dentō**	*light*
窓	**mado**	*window*
パーティー	**pātii**	*party*
テレビ	**terebi**	*television*
ひどい	**hidoi**	*terrible*
残念	**zannen**	*regrettable; too bad; a pity*

* The verb **suru** can combine with a number of nouns to make new verbs. These verbs are classified as irregular verbs (Group 3).

EXAMPLES: 旅行する **ryokō suru** (to travel)
卒業する **sotsugyō suru** (to graduate)
結婚する **kekkon suru** (to marry)

EXERCISES

A. Practice saying the following sentences in Japanese. Repeat the exercises until you no longer need to refer to the Japanese half.

1. | | | |
|---|---|---|
| *Shall we go together?* | **Issho ni ikimashō ka?** | 一緒に行きましょうか。 |
| *Shall we watch TV?* | **Terebi o mimashō ka?** | テレビを見ましょうか。 |
| *Shall we give the vase to Miss Toda?* | **Kabin o Toda-san ni agemashō ka?** | 花びんを戸田さんにあげましょうか。 |
| *Shall I open the window?* | **Mado o akemashō ka?** | 窓を開けましょうか。 |
| *Shall I turn on the light?* | **Dentō o tsukemashō ka?** | 電灯を点けましょうか。 |
| *Shall I turn off the light?* | **Dentō o keshimashō ka?** | 電灯を消しましょうか。 |
| *Shall I take a picture?* | **Shashin o torimashō ka?** | 写真を撮りましょうか。 |

2. *Let's go (for) sightseeing.* | **Kenbutsu ni ikimashō.** | 見物に行きましょう。
Let's invite Mr. Sato to the party. | **Satō-san o pātii ni shōtai shimashō.** | 佐藤さんをパーティーに招待しましょう。
Let's stay at this hotel. | **Kono hoteru ni tomarimashō.** | このホテルに泊まりましょう。
Let's rest for a while. | **Shibaraku yasumimashō.** | しばらく休みましょう。
Let's meet at the station. | **Eki de aimashō.** | 駅で会いましょう。

4. *What shall we drink?* | **Nani o nomimashō ka?** | 何を飲みましょうか。
Where shall we rest? | **Doko de yasumimashō ka?** | どこで休みましょうか。
When shall we meet? | **Itsu aimashō ka?** | いつ会いましょうか。
What time shall we return? | **Nan-ji ni kaerimashō ka?** | 何時に帰りましょうか。

5. *How are you?* | **O-genki desu ka?** | お元気ですか。
Fine, thanks. | **Arigatō, genki desu.** | ありがとう、元気です。
It's been a long time, hasn't it? | **Shibaraku desu ne.** | しばらくですね。
See you later. | **Jā, mata.** | じゃあ、また。

6. *That's wonderful, isn't it?* | **Subarashii desu ne.** | すばらしいですね。
That's terrible, isn't it? | **Hidoi desu ne.** | ひどいですね。
That's good, isn't it? | **Ii desu ne.** | いいですね。
That's too bad, isn't it? | **Zannen desu ne.** | 残念ですね。

B. Say the following sentences in Japanese.

1. Shall we stay at a Japanese inn?
2. Shall we go to Nara to see the large statue of Buddha?
3. Shall I give this book to Miss Yamada?
4. Shall I invite Mr. Wada to lunch?
5. Let's take pictures at the temple.
6. Let's meet in front of the movie theater.
7. It's been a long time (since we met), hasn't it?
8. That's wonderful, isn't it?
9. That's terrible, isn't it?
10. That's too bad, isn't it?

ANSWERS

B.

1. **Nihon no ryokan ni tomarimashō ka?** 日本の旅館に泊まりましょうか。
2. **Nara e Daibutsu o mi ni ikimashō ka?** 奈良へ大仏を見に行きましょうか。
3. **Yamada-san ni kono hon o agemashō ka?** 山田さんにこの本をあげましょうか。
4. **Wada-san o hiru-gohan ni shōtai shimashō ka?** 和田さんを昼ご飯に招待しましょうか。
5. **O-tera de shashin o torimashō.** お寺で写真を撮りましょう。
6. **Eiga-kan no mae de aimashō.** 映画館の前で会いましょう。
7. **Shibaraku desu ne.** しばらくですね。
8. **Subarashii desu ne.** すばらしいですね。
9. **Hidoi desu ne.** ひどいですね。
10. **Zannen desu ne.** 残念ですね。

LESSON 21

May I Sit Here?

VOCABULARY

Study these words and clearly pronounce them aloud. Then proceed to
the dialogue.

掛ける/座る	**kakeru/suwaru**	*to sit*
掛けて/座っても いいですか。	**Kakete/Suwatte mo ii desu ka?**[1]	*May I sit?*
吸う	**suu**	*to smoke*
着きます（着く）	**tsukimasu (tsuku)**	*arrive (to arrive)*
〜に着きます	**~ ni[2] tsukimasu**	*arrive at*
席	**seki**	*seat*
タバコ	**tabako**	*cigarette*
禁煙車	**kin'ensha**	*nonsmoking car*
ええ	**ē**	*(informal) yes*

DIALOGUE

Study the dialogue below. Practice until you no longer need to refer to the
Japanese half.

American : この席に掛けて／座ってもいいですか。
　　　　　　Kono seki ni kakete[1]/suwatte mo ii desu ka?
　　　　　　May I sit in this seat?
Japanese : ええ、どうぞ。
　　　　　　Ē, dōzo.
　　　　　　Yes, please.
American : この電車は何時に東京に着きますか。
　　　　　　Kono densha wa nan-ji ni Tokyō ni[2] tsukimasu ka?
　　　　　　What time does this train arrive at Tokyo?
Japanese : 午後六時頃着きます。
　　　　　　Gogo roku-ji goro tsukimasu.
　　　　　　It'll arrive around 6:00 P.M.

American ：ここでタバコを吸ってもいいですか。
Koko de tabako o sutte mo ii desu ka?
May I smoke here?

Japanese ：いいえ、吸わないで下さい。ここは禁煙車です。
Iie, suwanai de[3] kudasai. Koko wa kin'ensha desu.
No, please don't. This is a nonsmoking car.

 POINTS TO REMEMBER

1. **V-te mo ii desu ka?** May I do ~?/Is it all right to do ~?
   EXAMPLE: この本を読んでもいいですか。
   Kono hon o yonde mo ii desu ka?
   May I read this book?

2. NOUN + **ni tsukimasu**: arrive at NOUN
   Another usage of **ni** is to indicate an arrival point.
   EXAMPLE: 東京に着きます。
   Tōkyō ni tsukimasu.
   We will arrive at Tokyo.

3. **V-nai de kudasai**: Please don't ~ (*lit.,* Please do not give your ~ing.) How to make the **V-nai** forms is explained on page 116.
   EXAMPLE: 窓を開けて／開けないで下さい。
   Mado o akete/akenai de kudasai.
   Please open/don't open the window.

ADDITIONAL WORDS

Study these words and clearly pronounce them aloud. Then proceed to the dialogue.

脱ぐ	**nugu**	*to take off* (a coat)
置く	**oku**	*to put/leave* (a luggage)
止まる	**tomeru**	*to stop* (a car)
使う	**tsukau**	*to use*
箸	**hashi**	*chopsticks*
上着	**uwagi**	*jacket; coat*
荷物	**nimotsu**	*luggage*
待合室	**machiai-shitsu**	*waiting room*

The V-nai form

This is the negative form of Japanese verbs. The **V-nai** forms are formed as follows:

Regular Verbs (GROUP 1)

Drop the *-u* ending, and add *a* plus *-nai*.

EXAMPLES:

話す **hanasu**	+ **a** + ない **nai**	→	話さない **hanasanai**	*speak*
行く **iku**	+ **a** + ない **nai**	→	行かない **ikanai**	*go*
買う **ka(w)u**	+ **a** + ない **nai**	→	買わない **kawanai**	*buy*
待つ **matsu**	+ **a** + ない **nai**	→	待たない **matanai**	*wait*
脱ぐ **nugu**	+ **a** + ない **nai**	→	脱がない **nuganai**	*take off*
置く **oku**	+ **a** + ない **nai**	→	置かない **okanai**	*put*
押す **osu**	+ **a** + ない **nai**	→	押さない **osanai**	*push*
座る **suwaru**	+ **a** + ない **nai**	→	座わない **suwaranai**	*sit*
吸う **su(w)u**	+ **a** + ない **nai**	→	吸わない **suwanai**	*smoke*

Semi-regular Verbs (GROUP 2)

Drop the *-ru* ending and add *-nai*.

EXAMPLES:

掛ける **kakeru**	+ ない **nai**	→	掛けない **kakenai**	*sit*
食べる **taberu**	+ ない **nai**	→	食べない **tabenai**	*eat*
止める **tomeru**	+ ない **nai**	→	止めない **tomenai**	*stop*

Irregular Verbs (GROUP 3)

来る **kuru**	→	来ない **konai**	*come*
する **suru**	→	しない **shinai**	*do*

EXERCISES

A. Practice saying the following sentences in Japanese. Repeat the exercises until you no longer need to refer to the Japanese half.

1. *May I sit here on this seat?*	**Kono seki ni kakete/ suwatte mo ii desu ka?**	この席に掛けて／座ってもいいですか。
May I stop the car here?	**Koko ni kuruma o tomete mo ii desu ka?**	ここに車を止めてもいいですか。
May I put/leave the luggage here?	**Koko ni nimotsu o oite mo ii desu ka?**	ここに荷物を置いてもいいですか。
May I wait in the room?	**Heya de matte mo ii desu ka?**	部屋で待ってもいいですか。
May I take off the jacket?	**Uwagi o nuide mo ii desu ka?**	上着を脱いでもいいですか。

May I smoke a cigarette in the waiting room?	**Machiai-shitsu de tabako o sutte mo ii desu ka?**	待合室でタバコを吸ってもいいですか。
May I use these chopsticks?	**Kono hashi o tsukatte mo ii desu ka?**	この箸を使ってもいいですか。

2. *Please don't sit here.*   **Koko ni kakenai/ suwaranai de kudasai.**   ここに掛けない／座わないで下さい。

Please don't stop the car.	**Kuruma o tomenai de kudasai.**	車を止めないで下さい。
Please don't put/leave the luggage.	**Nimotsu o okanai de kudasai.**	荷物を置かないで下さい。
Please don't wait here.	**Koko de matanai de kudasai.**	ここで待たないで下さい。
Please don't take off your jacket.	**Uwagi o nuganai de kudasai.**	上着を脱がないで下さい。
Please don't smoke a cigarette.	**Tabako o suwanai de kudasai.**	タバコを吸わないで下さい。
Please don't go to the bank.	**Ginkō e ikanai de kudasai.**	銀行へ行かないで下さい。
Please don't speak in English.	**Ei-go de hanasanai de kudasai.**	英語で話さないで下さい。
Please don't buy souvenirs.	**O-miyage o kawanai de kudasai.**	お土産を買わないで下さい。
Please don't push this button.	**Kono botan o osanai de kudasai.**	このボタンを押さないで下さい。
Please don't read the newspaper.	**Shinbun o yomanai de kudasai.**	新聞を読まないで下さい。
Please don't eat breakfast.	**Asa-gohan o tabenai de kudasai.**	朝ご飯を食べないで下さい。
Please don't do any shopping.	**Kaimono o shinai de kudasai.**	買い物をしないで下さい。
Please don't come tonight.	**Kon-ban konai de kudasai.**	今晩来ないで下さい。

B. Answer the following questions using the cue words.

1. **Koko de tabako o sutte mo ii desu ka?**
   ここでタバコを吸ってもいいですか。
   (please do) **Ē,** _____

2. **Uwagi o nuide mo ii desu ka?**
   上着を脱いでもいいですか。
   (please do) **Ē,** _____

3. **Ei-go de hanashite mo ii desu ka?**
   英語で話してもいいですか。
   Iie, _____

4. **Kono botan o oshite mo ii desu ka?**
   このボタンを押してもいいですか。
   Iie, _____

5. **Koko ni nimotsu o oite mo ii desu ka?**
   ここ荷物を置いてもいいですか。
   Iie, _____

6. **Kyō bijutsu-kan e itte mo ii desu ka?**
   今日美術館へ行ってもいいですか。。
   Iie, _____

7. **Koko ni kuruma o tomete mo ii desu ka?**
   ここに車を止めてもいいですか。
   Iie, _____

8. **Ashita kaimono o shite mo ii desu ka?**
   あした買い物をしてもいいですか。
   Iie, _____

ANSWERS

B.
1. **Ē, dōzo.** ええ、どうぞ。
2. **Ē, dōzo.** ええ、どうぞ。
3. **Iie, hanasanai de kudasai.** いいえ、話さないで下さい。
4. **Iie, osanai de kudasai.** いいえ、押さないで下さい。
5. **Iie, okanai de kudasai.** いいえ、置かないで下さい。
6. **Iie, ikanai de kudasai.** いいえ、行かないで下さい。
7. **Iie, tomenai de kudasai.** いいえ、止めないで下さい。
8. **Iie, shinai de kudasai.** いいえ、しないで下さい。

Review Exercises

The following sentences were covered in Lessons 13 through 21. Repeat these practice sentences until you no longer need to refer to the Japanese half.

1. *Where are you going tomorrow?*   **Anata wa ashita doko e ikimasu ka?**   あなたはあしたどこ へ行きますか。
   I'm going to Kyoto.   **Kyōto e ikimasu.**   京都へ行きます。

2. *What time do you get up?*   **Nan-ji ni okimasu ka?**   何時に起きますか。
   I get up at 6:20.   **Roku-ji ni-jup-pun ni okimasu.**   六時二十分に起き ます。

3. *What will you do in the art museum?*   **Bijutsu-kan de nani o shimasu ka?**   美術館で何をしま すか。
   I'll see many pictures and photos.   **E to shashin o takusan mimasu.**   絵と写真をたくさん 見ます。

4. *What will you buy at the department store?*   **Depāto de nani o kaimasu ka?**   デパートで何を買い ますか。
   I'll buy a doll and a vase.   **Ningyō to kabin o kaimasu.**   人形と花びんを買 います。

5. *Will you also buy a sweater?*   **Sētā mo kaimasu ka?**   セーターも買います か。
   No, I won't buy a sweater.   **Iie, sētā wa kaimasen.**   いいえ、セーターは 買いません。

6. *Where do you drink coffee?*   **Doko de kōhii o nomimasu ka?**   どこでコーヒーを飲 みますか。
   I drink at a coffee shop.   **Kissaten de nomimasu.**   喫茶店で飲みます。

7. *Will you stay at a hotel?*

Hoteru ni tomarimasu ka?

ホテルに泊まります か。

No, I won't. I'll stay at a Japanese inn.

Iie, tomarimasen. Nihon no ryokan ni tomarimasu.

いいえ、泊まりませ ん。日本の旅館に 泊まります。

8. *Please show me that blue vase.*

Ano aoi kabin o misete kudasai.

あの青い花びんを 見せて下さい。

9. *This is a little (too) big, isn't it?*

Kore wa chotto ōkii desu ne.

これはちょっと大き いですね。

Please show me a smaller one.

Motto chiisai-no o misete kudasai.

もっと小さいのを見 せて下さい。

10. *How much is the white one?*

Shiroi-no wa ikura desu ka?

白いのはいくらです か。

It's 9,500 yen.

Kyū-sen-go-hyaku-en desu.

九千五百円です。

11. *Please give me the brown one.*

Chairo-no o kudasai.

茶色のを下さい。

Certainly, sir.

Kashikomarimashita.

かしこまりました。

12. *What did you do yesterday?*

Kinō nani o shimashita ka?

きのう何をしました か。

I went to Nara by a sightseeing bus.

Kankō-basu de Nara e ikimashita.

観光バスで奈良へ 行きました。

13. *What did you go there to do?*

Nani o shi ni ikimashita ka?

何をしに行きました か。

I went there to take pictures.

Shashin o tori ni ikimashita.

写真を撮りに行きま した。

14. *I bought a history book.*

Watashi wa rekishi no hon o kaimashita.

私は歴史の本を買 いました。

I also bought an economics book.

Keizai no hon mo kaimashita.

経済の本も買いま した。

15. *Can you speak Japanese?*

Anata wa Nihon-go ga dekimasu ka?

あなたは日本語が できますか。

Yes, I can. But, I am not good at it.

Hai, dekimasu. Demo, jōzu dewa arimasen.

はい、できます。で も上手ではありま せん。

16. *Can you teach French?*

Furansu-go o oshieru-koto ga dekimasu ka?

フランス語を教える事ができますか。

   No, I can't teach.

Iie, oshieru-koto ga dekimasen.

いいえ、教える事ができません。

17. *I am poor at golf.*

Watashi wa gorufu ga heta desu.

私はゴルフがへたです。

   I am poor at taking pictures.

Watashi wa shashin o toru-koto ga heta desu.

私は写真を撮る事がへたです。

18. *Miss Tanaka likes music.*

Tanaka-san wa ongaku ga suki desu.

田中さんは音楽が好きです。

   She doesn't like mountain climbing.

Yama-nobori wa suki dewa arimasen.

山のぼりは好きではありません。

19. *Mr. Sato likes swimming in the sea.*

Satō-san wa umi de oyogu-no ga suki desu.

斉藤さんは海で泳ぐのが好きです。

   He doesn't like writing letters.

Tegami o kaku-no wa suki dewa arimasen.

手紙を書くのは好きではありません。

20. *Where do you want to go on the weekend?*

Shū-matsu ni doko e iki-tai desu ka?

週末にどこへ行きたいですか。

   I want to go to a hot spring with my mother.

Haha to issho ni onsen e iki-tai desu.

母と一緒に温泉へ行きたいです。

21. *Do you want to go by airplane?*

Hikō-ki de iki-tai desu ka?

飛行機で行きたいですか。

   Yes. An airplane is faster.

Hai, hikō-ki no hō ga hayai desu.

はい、飛行機のほうが速いです。

22. *What do you want to eat at a restaurant?*

Resutoran de nani o tabe-tai desu ka?

レストランで何を食べたいですか。

   I want to eat sashimi and tenpura.

Sashimi to tenpura o tabe-tai desu.

刺身と天ぷらを食べたいです。

23. *What do you want to see in Kyoto?*

Kyōto de nani o mi-tai desu ka?

京都で何を見たいですか。

   I want to see Buddhist temples and Shinto shrines.

O-tera to jinja o mi-tai desu.

お寺と神社を見たいです。

24. *Please give me a round-trip ticket.* — **Ōfuku-kippu o kudasai.** — 往復切符を下さい。

Please say it once more. — **Mō ichido itte kudasai.** — もう一度言って下さい。

Please come tomorrow. — **Ashita kite kudasai.** — あした来て下さい。

Please put in money here. — **Koko ni o-kane o irete kudasai.** — ここにお金を入れて下さい。

Please look at the fare table. — **Unchin-hyō o mite kudasai.** — 運賃表を見て下さい。

25. *Please buy (it) at a vending machine.* — **Jidō-hanbai-ki de katte kudasai.** — 自動販売機で買って下さい。

Which vending machine is it? — **Dono jidō-hanbai-ki desu ka?** — どの自動販売機ですか。

26. *What shall we drink?* — **Nani o nomimashō ka?** — 何を飲みましょうか。

Let's drink beer. — **Biiru o nomimashō.** — ビールを飲みましょう。

27. *It's been a long time since we met, hasn't it?* — **Shibaraku desu ne.** — しばらくですね。

How are you? — **O-genki desu ka?** — お元気ですか。

Fine, thank you. — **Arigatō. Genki desu.** — ありがとう。元気です。

28. *Shall we go to see Kabuki this evening?* — **Kon-ban Kabuki o mi ni ikimashō ka?** — 今晩歌舞伎を見に行きましょうか。

That's wonderful! — **Subarashii desu ne!** — すばらしいですね！

29. *Shall I open the window?* — **Mado o akemashō ka?** — 窓を開けましょうか。

Yes, please open it. — **Ē, akete kudasai.** *or* **O-negai shimasu.** — ええ、開けてください。／お願いします。

30. *May I smoke here?* — **Koko de tabako o sutte mo ii desu ka?** — ここでタバコを吸ってもいいですか。

Yes, please. — **Ē, dōzo.** — ええ、どうぞ。

31. *May I speak in English?* — **Ei-go de hanashite mo ii desu ka?** — 英語で話してもいいですか。

No, please don't speak in English. — **Iie, Ei-go de hanasanai de kudasai.** — いいえ、英語で話さないで下さい。

APPENDIX 1: **Verb Conjugations**

All the verbs used in this book are listed below. The dictionary forms (except irregular verbs) are divided between the stem and the ending by a hyphen.

GROUP 1 (REGULAR VERBS)				
Dictionary form	**V-masu form**	**V-te form**	**V-nai form**	**English meaning**
ある **ar-u**	あります **arimasu**	あって **atte**	ない **nai***	*exist*
会う **a(w)-u**	会います **aimasu**	会って **atte**	会わない **awanai**	*meet*
入る **hair-u**	入ります **hairimasu**	入って **haitte**	入らない **hairanai**	*enter*
履く **hak-u**	履きます **hakimasu**	履いて **haite**	履かない **hakanai**	*wear*
話す **hanas-u**	話します **hanashimasu**	話して **hanashite**	話さない **hanasanai**	*speak*
弾く **hik-u**	弾きます **hikimasu**	弾いて **hiite**	弾かない **hikanai**	*play (piano)*
行く **ik-u**	行きます **ikimasu**	行って **itte***	行かない **ikanai**	*go*
急ぐ **isog-u**	急ぎます **isogimasu**	急いで **isoide**	急がない **isoganai**	*hurry*
言う **i(w)-u**	言います **iimasu**	言って **itte**	言わない **iwanai**	*say*
かぶる **kabur-u**	かぶります **kaburimasu**	かぶって **kabutte**	かぶらない **kaburanai**	*wear*
帰る **kaer-u**	帰ります **kaerimasu**	買って **kaette**	帰らない **kaeranai**	*return*
書く **kak-u**	書きます **kakimasu**	書いて **kaite**	書かない **kakanai**	*write*
買う **ka(w)-u**	買います **kaimasu**	買って **katte**	買わない **kawanai**	*buy*
消す **kes-u**	消します **keshimasu**	消して **keshite**	消さない **kesanai**	*turn off*
待つ **mats-u**	待ちます **machimasu**	待って **matte**	持たない **matanai**	*wait*

* Exceptions: ある **ar-u** → ない **nai** (*not* **aranai**);
行く **ik-u** → 行って **itte** (*not* **iite**)

GROUP 1 (REGULAR VERBS)				
Dictionary form	**V-masu form**	**V-te form**	**V-nai form**	**English meaning**
飲む **nom-u**	飲みます **nomimasu**	飲んで **nonde**	飲まない **nomanai**	*drink*
脱ぐ **nug-u**	脱ぎます **nugimasu**	脱いで **nuide**	脱がない **nuganai**	*take off*
置く **ok-u**	置きます **okimasu**	置いて **oite**	置かない **okanai**	*put*
押す **os-u**	押します **oshimasu**	押して **oshite**	押さない **osanai**	*push*
泳ぐ **oyog-u**	泳ぎます **oyogimasu**	泳いで **oyoide**	泳がない **oyoganai**	*swim*
死ぬ **shin-u**	死にます **shinimasu**	死んで **shinde**	死なない **shinanai**	*die*
吸う **su(w)-u**	吸います **suimasu**	吸って **sutte**	吸わない **suwanai**	*smoke*
座る **suwar-u**	座ります **suwarimasu**	座って **suwatte**	座わない **suwarani**	*sit*
立つ **tats-u**	立ちます **tachimasu**	立って **tatte**	立たない **tatanai**	*stand*
止まる **tomar-u**	止まります **tomarimasu**	止まって **tomatte**	止まらない **tomaranai**	*stay*
撮る **tor-u**	撮ります **torimasu**	撮って **totte**	撮らない **toranai**	*take (a picture)*
使う **tsuka(w)-u**	使います **tsukaimasu**	使って **tsukatte**	使わない **tsukawanai**	*use*
着く **tsuk-u**	着きます **tsukimasu**	着いて **tsuite**	着かない **tsukanai**	*arrive*
作る **tsukur-u**	作ります **tsukurimasu**	作って **tsukutte**	作らない **tsukuranai**	*make*
歌う **uta(w)-u**	歌います **utaimasu**	歌って **utatte**	歌わない **utawanai**	*sing*
休む **yasum-u**	休みます **yasumimasu**	休んで **yasunde**	休まない **yasumanai**	*rest*
呼ぶ **yob-u**	呼びます **yobimasu**	呼んで **yonde**	呼ばない **yobanai**	*call*
読む **yom-u**	読みます **yomimasu**	読んで **yonde**	読まない **yomanai**	*read*

GROUP 2 (SEMI-REGULAR VERBS)

Dictionary form	V-masu form	V-te form	V-nai form	English meaning
あげる **age-ru**	あげます **agemasu**	あげて **agete**	あげない **agenai**	*give*
開ける **ake-ru**	開けます **akemasu**	開けて **akete**	開けない **akenai**	*open*
集める **atsume-ru**	集めます **atsumemasu**	集めて **atsumete**	集めない **atsumenai**	*collect*
できる **deki-ru**	できます **dekimasu**	できて **dekite**	できない **dekinai**	*be possible*
入れる **ire-ru**	入れます **iremasu**	入れて **irete**	入れない **irenai**	*put in*
いる **i-ru**	います **imasu**	いて **ite**	いない **inai**	*exist*
掛ける **kake-ru**	掛けます **kakemasu**	掛けて **kakete**	掛けない **kakenai**	*sit*
着る **ki-ru**	着ます **kimasu**	着て **kite**	着ない **kinai**	*wear*
見る **mi-ru**	見ます **mimasu**	見て **mite**	見ない **minai**	*see*
見せる **mise-ru**	見せます **misemasu**	見せて **misete**	見せない **misenai**	*show*
寝る **ne-ru**	寝ます **nemasu**	寝て **nete**	寝ない **nenai**	*sleep*
起きる **oki-ru**	起きます **okimasu**	起きて **okite**	起きない **okinai**	*get up*
教える **oshie-ru**	教えます **oshiemasu**	教えて **oshiete**	教えない **oshienai**	*teach*
食べる **tabe-ru**	食べます **tabemasu**	食べて **tabete**	食べない **tabenai**	*eat*
止める **tome-ru**	止めます **tomemasu**	止めて **tomete**	止めない **tomenai**	*stop*
点ける **tsuke-ru**	点けます **tsukemasu**	点けて **tsukete**	点けない **tsukenai**	*turn on*

GROUP 3 (IRREGULAR VERBS)				
Dictionary form	V-masu form	V-te form	V-nai form	English meaning
来る **kuru**	来ます **kimasu**	来て **kite**	来ない **konai**	*come*
する **suru**	します **shimasu**	して **shite**	しない **shinai**	*do*
結婚する **kekkon suru**	結婚します **kekkon shimasu**	結婚して **kekkon shite**	結婚しない **kekkon shinai**	*marry*
旅行する **ryokō suru**	旅行します **ryokō shimasu**	旅行して **ryokō shite**	旅行しない **ryokō shinai**	*travel*
招待する **shōtai suru**	招待します **shōtai shimasu**	招待して **shōtai shite**	招待しない **shōtai shinai**	*invite*
卒業する **sotsugyō suru**	卒業します **sotsugyō shimasu**	卒業して **sotsugyō shite**	卒業しない **sotsugyō shinai**	*graduate*

APPENDIX 2: **Particles**

Japanese particles indicate the relationship of the preceding word(s) to either the following word or the rest of the sentence. All the particles used in this book are listed below alphabetically.

DE

1. NOUN + de: by means of/in/with NOUN
   De is used to indicate an instrument or means.
   EXAMPLES: タクシーで十五分です。
   > **Takushii de jū-go-fun gurai desu.**
   > *It's about 15 minutes by taxi.* (Lesson 5)
   > 英語で話してください。
   > **Ei-go de hanashite kudasai.**
   > *Please speak in English.* (Lesson 19)

2. NOUN + de: at/in NOUN
   De is added to a place-related noun to indicate where an action takes place.
   EXAMPLE: 部屋で食べます。
   > **Heya de tabemasu.**
   > *I eat in the room.* (Lesson 13)

E

NOUN + e: to NOUN
E is used to indicate direction.
> EXAMPLE: 私は京都／銀行へ行きます。
> **Watashi wa Kyōto/ginkō e ikimasu.**
> *I am going to Kyoto/the bank.* (Lesson 13)

GA

NOUN + ga
Ga is a subject marker and indicates that the preceding noun is a subject of the sentence.
> EXAMPLE: レストランがあります。
> **Resutoran ga arimasu.**
> *There is a restaurant./A restaurant exists.* (Lesson 9)

Wa also indicates the subject of a sentence, but **wa** indicates that the subject preceding it is the topic of the sentence—thus, **wa** can be translated "as for ~."

> EXAMPLE: 本があります。
>> **Hon ga arimasu.**
>> *There is a book.*
>> 本は私の(本)です。
>> **Hon _wa_ watashi no (hon) desu.**
>> _As for_ the book, it is mine. (Lesson 9)

GURAI
NUMBER + gurai

Gurai is added to a number to indicate an approximate quantity.

> EXAMPLE: 十五分ぐらいです。
>> **Jū-go-fun _gurai_ desu.**
>> *It's _about_ 15 minutes.* (Lesson 5)

KA
SENTENCE + ka

Used as a question marker, **ka** at the end of a sentence turns it into a question.

> EXAMPLE: あの人は誰ですか。
>> **Ano hito wa dare desu _ka_?**
>> *Who is that person?* (Lesson 1)

KARA
NOUN + kara: from NOUN

Kara is used to indicate a starting point in place and time.

> EXAMPLES: 東京から大阪まで三時間です。
>> **Tōkyō _kara_ Ōsaka made san-jikan desu.**
>> _From_ Tokyo to Osaka it's 3 hours.
>> 会社は九時からです。
>> **Kaisha wa ku-ji _kara_ desu.**
>> *The company is (open) _from_ 9:00.* (Lesson 5)

MADE
NOUN + made: to/till NOUN

Made is used to indicate an ending point in place and time.

> EXAMPLES: 東京駅までです。
>> **Tōkyō Eki _made_ desu.**
>> _To_ Tokyo Station. (Lesson 2)

会社は五時までです。

Kaisha wa go-ji <u>made</u> desu.

The company is (open) <u>till</u> 5:00.

会議は午前八時から九時までです。

Kaigi wa gozen hachi-ji kara ku-ji <u>made</u> desu.

The conference will be from 8:00 A.M. <u>to</u> 9:00. (Lesson 5)

MO

NOUN + **mo**: NOUN also/too

Mo refers to the word immediately preceding it and gives the meaning "also" or "too." It replaces **o** (an object marker) and **wa** (a topic or subject marker).

EXAMPLES: 本を買いました。花びんも買いました。

Hon o kaimashita. Kabin <u>mo</u> kaimashita.

I bought a book. I <u>also</u> bought a flower vase.

父も医者です。

Chichi <u>mo</u> isha desu.

My father <u>also</u> is a doctor. (Lesson 15)

NE

SENTENCE + **ne**

Ne is an end-of-a-sentence particle meaning "isn't it?" or "aren't you?"

EXAMPLE: 「ひかり」ですね。

Hikari desu <u>ne</u>.

Hikari, <u>isn't it?</u> (Lesson 4)

NI

1. NOUN + **ni**: at/in/on NOUN

   Ni, when added to a noun, indicates the location of something.

   EXAMPLE: ホテルにカメラ屋があります。

   Hoteru <u>ni</u> kamera-ya ga arimasu.

   There is a camera shop <u>in</u> the hotel. (Lesson 9)

2. NOUN + **ni**: at/on NOUN

   Ni, when added to a time-related noun, indicates a point in time.

   EXAMPLE: 八時に行きます。土曜日に帰ります。

   Hachi-ji <u>ni</u> ikimasu. Do-yōbi <u>ni</u> kaerimasu.

   I'll go <u>at</u> 8:00. I'll return <u>on</u> Saturday. (Lesson 13)

3. NOUN + **ni**: to NOUN

   Ni, as an indirect object marker, is added to an indirect object of a verb.

   EXAMPLE: 友達に手紙を書きました。

   Tomodachi <u>ni</u> tegami o kakimashita.

   I wrote a letter <u>to</u> my friend. (Lesson 17)

4a. **V(-masu) + ni + MOTION VERB**: go/come/return to do
This expression is used only with motion verbs such as *go*, *come*, and *return*, and indicates purpose. **Ni** is added to a verb from which the *-masu* ending has been dropped.

> EXAMPLE: 私は映画を見に行きます。
>> **Watashi wa eiga o mi ni ikimasu.**
>> *I'll go to see a movie.* (Lesson 15)

4b. **NOUN + ni + MOTION VERB**: go/come/return for NOUN
Ni is added to an "activity" noun such as sightseeing or lunch, and indicates purpose.

> EXAMPLE: 佐藤さんは昼ご飯／見物に行きます。
>> **Satō-san wa hiru-gohan/kenbutsu ni ikimasu.**
>> *Mr. Sato will go for lunch/sightseeing.* (Lesson 15)

5. **NOUN + ni tsukimasu**: arrive at NOUN
Ni is used to indicate an arrival point.

> EXAMPLE: 私は東京に着きます。
>> **Watashi wa Tōkyō ni tsukimasu.**
>> *I will arrive at Tokyo.* (Lesson 21)

6. **NOUN + ni hairimasu**: enter NOUN
Ni is used to indicate the place where a person moves into.

> EXAMPLE: 部屋に入りました。
>> **Heya ni hairimashita.**
>> *I entered the room.* (Lesson 19)

NO

1. **NOUN (A) + no + NOUN (B)**: NOUN (B) of NOUN (A)
[NOUN (A) + no] modifies NOUN (B)

> EXAMPLE: 朝日新聞の記者。
>> **Asahi Shinbun no kisha**
>> *a reporter for the Asahi Newspaper* (Lesson 1)

When NOUN (A) is a person, NOUN (A) + no indicates the possessive form—my, your, his, her, Mr. X's, etc.

> EXAMPLE: 今日は山田さんの誕生日です。
>> **Kyō wa Yamada-san no tanjō-bi desu.**
>> *Today is Mr. Yamada's birthday.* (Lesson 6)

2. **ADJECTIVE/NOUN + no**: ADJECTIVE/NOUN one
No is added to an adjective or a noun to make a modified pronoun.

> EXAMPLES: 青いのを見せて下さい。
>> **Aoi-no o misete kudasai.**
>> *Please show me a blue one.*
>> 茶色のを下さい。
>> **Chairo-no o kudasai.**
>> *Please give me a brown one.* (Lesson 14)

3. (NOUN + **wa**) + [VERB + **no**] + **ga suki desu**: NOUN like [GERUND]
   No is used to make a gerund out of a verb.
   > EXAMPLE: 福田さんは泳ぐのが好きです。
   >> **Fukuda-san wa <u>oyogu-no</u> ga suki desu.**
   >> *Mr. Fukuda likes <u>swimming</u>.* (Lesson 17)

   Note that [VERB + **koto**] can also be used.
   > EXAMPLE: 父は手紙を書くの／書く事が好きです。
   >> **Chichi wa tegami o <u>kaku-no/kaku-koto</u> ga suki desu.**
   >> *My father likes <u>writing</u> letters.* (Lesson 17)

O

NOUN + **o shimasu**: ~ do/will do NOUN

O is an object marker added to a noun that is the direct object of a verb.
> EXAMPLE: 本を読みます。
>> **Hon <u>o</u> yomimasu.**
>> *I read <u>a book</u>.* (Lesson 13)

TO

1. NOUN + **to issho**: together with NOUN
   > EXAMPLE: 田中さんと一緒です。
   >> **Tanaka-san to issho desu.**
   >> *I'll be <u>with Mr. Tanaka</u>.* (Lesson 8)
2. NOUN + **to** + NOUN: NOUN and NOUN
   To is used to connect two nouns.
   > EXAMPLE: 奈良と京都へ行きました。
   >> **<u>Nara to Kyōto</u> e ikimashita.**
   >> *I went to <u>Nara and Kyoto</u>.* (Lesson 17)

WA

1. NOUN + **wa**: As for NOUN
   Wa is a topic marker that indicates the topic (or subject) of a sentence. A topic can be anything—a person, a thing, the weather—that comes at the beginning of the sentence.
   This topic is then followed by **wa**.
   > EXAMPLE: あの人は記者です。
   >> **Ano hito <u>wa</u> kisha desu.**
   >> *That person <u>is</u> a reporter.* (Lesson 1)

2. NOUN + **wa arimasen/imasen**: There is/are no NOUN.

    Wa is frequently used in negative sentences to contrast a negative idea with a positive idea.

    > EXAMPLES: 灰皿があります。マッチはありません。
    >
    > **Haizara ga arimasu. Matchi _wa arimasen_.**
    >
    > *There are ashtrays. [But] There are _no_ matches.*
    > (Lesson 10)
    >
    > 女の人はいません。
    >
    > **Onna no hito _wa imasen_.**
    >
    > *There are _no_ women.* (Lesson 11)
    >
    > 私は歌を歌うのは好きではありません。
    >
    > **Watashi wa uta o utau-no wa suki _dewa arimasen_.**
    >
    > *I _don't_ like singing songs.* (Lesson 17)

3a. **Wa** (a topic marker) and **ga** (a subject marker) can be used in the same sentence.

    (NOUN + **wa**) + [SOMETHING] + **ga dekimasu**: NOUN can do [SOMETHING]

    > EXAMPLE: カーターさんは日本語ができます。
    >
    > **Kātā-san _wa_ Nihon-go _ga_ dekimasu.**
    >
    > *Mr. Carter _can speak_ Japanese.* (*lit.*, As for Mr. Carter, Japanese is possible.) (Lesson 16)

3b. (NOUN + **wa**) + [SOMETHING] + **ga suki desu**: NOUN like [SOMETHING]

    > EXAMPLE: 母は花が好きです。
    >
    > **Haha _wa_ hana _ga suki_ desu.**
    >
    > *My mother _likes_ flowers.* (Lesson 17)

    Note that when the subject happens to be the topic, **wa** is used. (*see* **wa**, **1**)

YO

SENTENCE + **yo**

Yo is an end-of-a-sentence particle meaning "I assure you."

> EXAMPLE: あそこですよ。
>
> **Asoko desu _yo_.**
>
> *It's over there, _I tell you_.* (Lesson 4)

APPENDIX 3: **Counters**

Japanese has a unique counting system. When counting things, what counters (or counter suffixes) you must add to numerals depends upon the objects. Besides those used in the book, there are many other counters. The following are some of the most common ones.

	本 **long objects**	冊 **bound objects**	枚 **flat objects**	足 **footwear**
1	一本 **ip-pon**	一冊 **is-satsu**	一枚 **ichi-mai**	一足 **is-soku**
2	二本 **ni-hon**	二冊 **ni-satsu**	二枚 **ni-mai**	二足 **ni-soku**
3	三本 **san-bon**	三冊 **san-satsu**	三枚 **san-mai**	三足 **san-zoku**
4	四本 **yon-hon**	四冊 **yon-satsu**	四枚 **yo-mai/yon-mai**	四足 **yon-soku**
5	五本 **go-hon**	五冊 **go-satsu**	五枚 **go-mai**	五足 **go-soku**
6	六本 **rop-pon**	六冊 **roku-satsu**	六枚 **roku-mai**	六足 **roku-soku**
7	七本 **nana-hon**	七冊 **nana-satsu**	七枚 **nana-mai**	七足 **nana-soku**
8	八本 **hachi-hon/ hap-pon**	八冊 **has-satsu**	八枚 **hachi-mai**	八足 **has-soku**
9	九本 **kyū-hon**	九冊 **kyū-satsu**	九枚 **kyū-mai**	九足 **kyū-soku**
10	十本 **jup-pon/jip-pon**	十冊 **jus-satsu/ jis-satsu**	十枚 **jū-mai**	十足 **jus-soku/jis-soku**

EXAMPLES:

1. 鉛筆が何本ありますか。   **Enpitsu ga nan-bon arimasu ka?**   *How many pencils are there?*

   五本あります。   **Go-hon arimasu.**   *There are five.*

2. 本が何冊ありますか。   **Hon ga nan-satsu arimasu ka?**   *How many books are there?*

   九冊あります。   **Kyū-satsu arimasu.**   *There are nine.*

3. 紙が何枚ありますか。 **Kami ga nan-mai arimasu ka?** *How many sheets of paper are there?*

　八枚あります。 **Hachi-mai arimasu.** *There are eight.*

4. 靴が何足ありますか。 **Kutsu ga nan-zoku arimasu ka?** *How many pairs of shoes are there?*

　二足あります。 **Ni-soku arimasu.** *There are two pairs.*

Vocabulary

Listed here are all the words used in this book, as well as the lessons or appendixes in which the words first appeared. Verbs are given in their dictionary forms.

Japanese–English

ā	ああ	*oh*	L 3
Ā, sō desu ka.	ああ、そうですか。	*Oh, I see./Is that so?*	L 3
ageru	あげる	*to give*	L 20
akai	赤い	*red*	L 14
akeru	開ける	*to open*	L 20
aki	秋	*autumn*	L 17
Amerika	アメリカ	*America*	L 1
Amerika-jin	アメリカ人	*American (person)*	L 2
Amerika no kata	アメリカの方	*person of America (polite)*	L 2
anata	あなた	*you*	L 2
anata no	あなたの	*your*	L 6
ano	あの	*that*	L 1
ano hito	あの人	*that person*	L 1
aoi	青い	*blue*	L 14
aoi-no	青いの	*blue one*	L 14
are	あれ	*that (one)*	L 2
Arigatō.	ありがとう	*Thank you.*	L 3
aru	ある	*exist; there is/are (for inanimate objects)*	L 9
asa	朝	*morning*	L 13
asa-gohan	朝ご飯	*breakfast*	L 13
Asahi Shinbun	朝日新聞	*Asahi Newspaper*	L 1
ashita	あした	*tomorrow*	L 6

asoko	あそこ	*over there*	L 3
Atami	熱海	(famous hot spring resort)	L 18
atatakai	暖かい	*warm*	L 8
atsui	熱い／暑い	*hot*	L 8
atsumeru	集める	*to collect*	L 17
au	会う	*to meet*	L 20
ban	晩	*evening; night*	L 13
-ban	番	(a suffix used for ordinal numbers)	L 4
ban-gohan	晩ご飯	*supper*	L 13
basu	バス	*bus*	L 5
benri	便利	*convenient*	L 18
-bi	日	(a suffix used for special days. When added to a noun, **hi**, meaning "day," changes to **bi**.)	L 6
biiru	ビール	*beer*	L 9
bijutsu-kan	美術館	*art museum*	L 13
bōshi	帽子	*hat; cap*	L 18
botan	ボタン	*button*	L 19
byōin	病院	*hospital*	L 3
chairo	茶色	*brown*	L 14
chichi	父	*(my) father*	L 8
chiisai-no	小さいの	*small one*	L 14
chika	地下	*basement*	L 9
chikai	近い	*near*	L 5
chika-tetsu	地下鉄	*subway*	L 5
chotto	ちょっと	*a little*	L 14
daibutsu	大仏	*a large statue of Buddha*	L 15
daigaku	大学	*college; university*	L 19
dare	誰	*who*	L 1
de	で	*by means of; in; with at; in (place)*	L 5 / L 13
dekiru	できる	*can; is able to; is possible*	L 16
demo	でも	*but*	L 16
densha	電車	*train*	L 4
dentō	電灯	*light*	L 20
denwa	電話	*telephone*	L 3
depāto	デパート	*department store*	L 5
deshita	でした	*was; were*	L 6
desu	です	*is; am; are*	L 1
dewa arimasen	ではありません	*is/am/are not*	L 7
dewa arimasen deshita	ではありません でした	*was/were not*	L 7

dō	どう	*how*	L 18
dōbutsu	動物	*animal*	L 17
Dō-itashimashite.	どういたしまして。	*You are welcome.*	L 3
Doitsu	ドイツ	*Germany*	L 2
Doitsu-go	ドイツ語	*German language*	L 16
Doitsu-jin	ドイツ人	*German (person)*	L 2
doko	どこ	*where*	L 2
Dōmo arigatō.	どうもありがとう。	*Thank you.*	L 4
dono	どの	*which*	L 19
dore	どれ	*which (one)*	L 19
Do-yōbi	土曜日	*Saturday*	L 7
dōzo	どうぞ	*please*	L 1
Dōzo yoroshiku.	どうぞよろしく。	*Glad to meet you.*	L 1
e	絵	*painting*	L 14
e	へ	*to (a direction marker)*	L 13
ē	ええ	*yes (informal)*	L 21
ebi	エビ	*shrimp*	L 9
eiga-kan	映画館	*movie theater*	L 3
Ei-go	英語	*English language*	L 16
Ei-go de	英語で	*in English*	L 19
eigyō-bu	営業部	*sales department*	L 11
eki	駅	*station*	L 2
-en	円	*(a suffix used for currency)*	L 14
enpitsu	えんぴつ	*pencil*	A 3
Fukuda	福田	*(a family name)*	L 16
-fun	分	*(a suffix used for minutes)*	L 4
fune	船	*ship*	L 5
Furansu	フランス	*France*	L 2
Furansu-go	フランス語	*French language*	L 16
Furansu-jin	フランス人	*French (person)*	L 2
futari	二人	*2 persons*	L 11
futatsu	二つ	*two*	L 10
futsuka	二日	*the 2nd*	L 6
fuyu	冬	*winter*	L 17
ga	が	*(a subject marker)*	L 9
gakkō	学校	*school*	L 3
-gatsu	月	*(a suffix used for the names of the months)*	L 8
genki	元気	*healthy; fine*	L 1
-getsu	月	*month*	L 8
Getsu-yōbi	月曜日	*Monday*	L 7
ginkō	銀行	*bank*	L 2
go	五	*5*	L 4
-go	語	*(a suffix used for languages)*	L 16

Gochisō-sama deshita.	ごちそうさまでした。	*It was delicious.*	L 1
Go-gatsu	五月	*May*	L 8
gogo	午後	*P.M. (afternoon)*	L 4
gohan	ご飯	*meal; cooked rice*	L 13
go-jū	五十	*50*	L 4
~ goro	頃	*about ~ (an approximate point in time)*	L 20
gorufu	ゴルフ	*golf*	L 16
gozaimasu	ございます	*exist; there is/are* (polite)	L 9
gozen	午前	*A.M. (morning)*	L 4
~ gurai	ぐらい	*about ~* (an approximate quantity)	L 5
hachi	八	*8*	L 4
Hachi-gatsu	八月	*August*	L 8
hachi-jū	八十	*80*	L 4
haha	母	*(my) mother*	L 8
hai	はい	*yes*	L 1
hairu	入る	*to enter*	L 19
haizara	灰皿	*ashtray*	L 10
Hajimemashite.	はじめまして。	*How do you do?*	L 1
Hakata-yuki	博多行き	*(train) for Hakata*	L 4
haku	履く	*to wear (shoes)*	L 18
hako	箱	*box*	L 10
-han	半	*half* (suffix for half an hour)	L 4
hanasu	話す	*to speak*	L 16
hana-ya	花屋	*flower shop*	L 3
haru	春	*spring*	L 17
hashi	箸	*chopsticks*	L 21
hayai	速い	*fast*	L 18
heta	へた	*poor; unskillful*	L 16
heya	部屋	*room*	L 10
hidari	左	*left*	L 3
hidoi	ひどい	*terrible*	L 20
Hikari	ひかり	(name of a super express Shinkansen)	L 4
hikō-ki	飛行機	*airplane*	L 5
hiku	弾く	*to play (the piano)*	L 18
hima	暇	*free (not busy)*	L 20
hiru	昼	*noon; daytime*	L 13
hiru-gohan	昼ご飯	*lunch*	L 13
Hiru-san	ヒルさん	*Mr./Mrs./Miss Hill*	L 20
hisho	秘書	*secretary*	L 11
hito	人	*person*	L 1
hitori	一人	*1 person; alone*	L 11 / L 8

hitotsu	一つ	*one*	L 10
hō	方	*side* (used for comparison)	L 18
hon	本	*book*	L 3
-hon	本	(a counter used for long objects)	A 3
hon-ya	本屋	*bookstore*	L 3
hoteru	ホテル	*hotel*	L 2
hyaku	百	*100*	L 14
hyō	表	*table; schedule*	L 19
ichi	一	*1*	L 4
Ichi-gatsu	一月	*January*	L 8
ichi-man	一万	*10,000*	L 14
Igirisu	イギリス	*England*	L 2
Igirisu-jin	イギリス人	*English (person)*	L 2
ii	いい	*good*	L 8
iie	いいえ	*no*	L 2
ikaga	いかが	*how (about)*	L 14
iku	行く	*to go*	L 13
ikura	いくら	*how much*	L 14
ikutsu	いくつ	*how many (things)*	L 10
ima	今	*now*	L 4
Irasshaimase.	いらっしゃいませ。	*Welcome.*	L 14
ireru	入れる	*to put in*	L 19
iru	いる	*to exist; there is/are* (for animate objects)	L 11
isha	医者	*doctor*	L 1
isogashii	忙しい	*busy*	L 20
isogu	急ぐ	*to hurry*	L 19
isu	椅子	*chair*	L 10
Itadakimasu.	いただきます。	*I will receive/have.*	L 1
itsu	いつ	*when*	L 8
itsuka	いつか	*the 5th*	L 6
itsutsu	五つ	*five*	L 10
iu	言う	*to say*	L 19
Jā, mata.	じゃあ、また。	*See you later/again.*	L 20
-ji	時	(a suffix used for o'clock/ hours)	L 4
jidō-hanbai-ki	自動販売機	*vending machine*	L 19
-jikan	時間	(a suffix used for hours)	L 5
-jin	人	(a suffix used for nationality)	L 2
jinja	神社	*Shinto shrine*	L 15
jisho	辞書	*dictionary*	L 19
jōzu	上手	*good; skillful*	L 16

jū	十	*10*	L 4
Jū-gatsu	十月	*October*	L 8
Jū-ichi-gatsu	十一月	*November*	L 8
Jū-ni-gatsu	十二月	*December*	L 8
ka	か	(a question marker)	L 1
kabin	花びん	*vase*	L 14
Kabuki	歌舞伎	*traditional Japanese drama*	L 2
Kabuki-za	歌舞伎座	*the Kabuki Theater*	L 2
kaburu	かぶる	*to wear (a hat)*	L 18
kaeru	帰る	*return (to a place)*	L 13
-kai	階	(a suffix used for floors)	L 9
kaigi	会議	*conference*	L 5
kaigi-shitsu	会議室	*conference room*	L 10
kaimono	買い物	*shopping*	L 7
kaisha	会社	*company*	L 5
kaisha-in	会社員	*company employee*	L 1
kakeru	掛ける	*to sit*	L 21
kaku	書く	*to write*	L 17
kamera-ya	カメラ屋	*camera shop*	L 9
kami	紙	*paper*	A 3
kangoshi	看護師	*nurse*	L 1
kankō-basu	観光バス	*sightseeing bus*	L 15
kara	から	*from*	L 5
~ kara ~ made	〜から〜まで	*from ~ to/till ~*	L 5
Kashikomari-mashita.	かしこまりました。	*Certainly, sir/ma'am.*	L 9
kata	方	*person (polite)*	L 2
katamichi	片道	*one-way*	L 19
Kātā-san	カーターさん	*Mr./Mrs./Miss Carter*	L 1
Katō	加藤	(a family name)	L 8
kau	買う	*to buy*	L 13
Ka-yōbi	火曜日	*Tuesday*	L 7
keizai	経済	*economics*	L 15
kekkon-shiki	結婚式	*wedding*	L 6
kekkon suru	結婚する	*to marry*	L 20
kenbutsu	見物	*sightseeing*	L 15
kesa	今朝	*this morning*	L 15
kesu	消す	*to turn off (the light)*	L 20
-ki	機	(a suffix used for machines)	L 19
Kimura	木村	(a family name)	L 7
kin'ensha	禁煙車	*nonsmoking car*	L 21
kinō	きのう	*yesterday*	L 6
Kin-yōbi	金曜日	*Friday*	L 7
kippu	切符	*ticket*	L 19
kirei	きれい	*pretty*	L 18
kiru	着る	*to wear (a sweater)*	L 18

kisha	記者	*reporter*	L 1
kissaten	喫茶店	*coffee shop*	L 9
kitte	切手	*stamp*	L 17
kō-cha	紅茶	*black tea*	L 13
kochira	こちら	*this person/thing*	L 1
Kodama	こだま	(name of a limited express *Shinkansen*)	L 5
kōen	公園	*park*	L 15
kōhii	コーヒー	*coffee*	L 13
koko	ここ	*here*	L 3
kokonoka	九日	*the 9th*	L 6
kokonotsu	九つ	*nine*	L 10
kon-ban	今晩	*tonight; this evening*	L 20
Konbanwa.	こんばんは。	*Good evening.*	L 1
kon-getsu	今月	*this month*	L 8
Konnichiwa.	こんにちは。	*Good day/afternoon.*	L 1
kono	この	*this*	L 2
konsāto	コンサート	*concert*	L 5
kon-shū	今週	*this week*	L 7
koppu	コップ	*cup; glass*	L 10
kore	これ	*this (one)*	L 2
ku	九	*9*	L 4
kudamono	果物	*fruit*	L 15
kudasai	下さい	*please; please give me*	L 14
Ku-gatsu	九月	*September*	L 8
kūkō	空港	*airport*	L 2
kuroi	黒い	*black*	L 14
kuru	来る	*to come*	L 16
kuruma	車	*car*	L 15
kutsu	靴	*shoes*	L 18
kyō	今日	*today*	L 6
kyo-nen	去年	*last year*	L 15
Kyōto	京都	*Kyoto (old capital of Japan)*	L 13
kyū	九	*9*	L 4
kyū-jū	九十	*90*	L 4
machiai-shitsu	待合室	*waiting room*	L 21
made	まで	*to*	L 2
mado	窓	*window*	L 20
mae	前	*front*	L 3
maguro	マグロ	*tuna*	L 9
maguro no sashimi	マグロの刺身	*sliced raw tuna*	L 9
-mai	枚	(a counter used for flat objects)	A 3
mata	また	*again*	L 20
matchi	マッチ	*match*	L 10

matsu	待つ	*to wait*	L 19
-matsu	末	*the end of ~*	L 18
mazu	まず	*first; to begin with*	L 19
michi	道	*road; street*	L 19
migi	右	*right*	L 3
mikka	三日	*the 3rd*	L 6
minna	みんな	*all*	L 11
miru	見る	*to see; watch; look*	L 13
mise	店	*store; shop*	L 19
miseru	見せる	*to show*	L 14
misete kudasai	見せて下さい	*please show*	L 14
mittsu	三つ	*three*	L 10
mo	も	*also; too*	L 15
mo ichido	もう一度	*once more*	L 19
Moku-yōbi	木曜日	*Thursday*	L 7
Moshi-moshi.	もしもし	*Hello (on the telephone)*	L 20
motto	もっと	*more*	L 14
motto chiisai-no	もっと小さいの	*smaller one*	L 14
motto yukkuri	もっとゆっくり	*slower*	L 19
muika	六日	*the 6th*	L 6
Murata	村田	(a family name)	L 15
muttsu	六つ	*six*	L 10
Nakano	中野	(a family name)	L 17
nana	七	*7*	L 4
nana-jū	七十	*70*	L 4
nanatsu	七つ	*seven*	L 10
nan-ban-sen	何番線	*what track*	L 4
nan-bon	何本	*how many (long objects)*	A 3
nan(i)	何	*what*	L 2
nan-ji	何時	*what time*	L 4
nan-jikan	何時間	*how many hours*	L 5
nan-mai	何枚	*how many (sheets)*	A 3
nan-nichi	何日	*what day (of the month)*	L 6
nan-nin	何人	*how many persons*	L 11
nan no	何の	*what kind of*	L 9
nanoka	七日	*the 7th*	L 6
nan-pun	何分	*how many minutes*	L 5
nan-satsu	何冊	*how many (volumes)*	A 3
nan-yōbi	何曜日	*what day of the week*	L 7
nan-zoku	何足	*how many (pairs)*	A 3
Nara	奈良	(a city name)	L 15
natsu	夏	*summer*	L 17
~ ne.	ね	*~ isn't it?*	L 4
-nen	年	(a suffix used for years)	L 15
neru	寝る	*to sleep; go to bed*	L 13
ni	二	*2*	L 4

ni	に	*to (do); for (the purpose of)*	L 15
		at; in; on (place)	L 9
		at; on (time)	L 13
		to (an indirect object marker)	L 17
ni hairu	に入る	*to enter (a room)*	L 19
ni tsuku	に着く	*to arrive at*	L 21
-nichi	日	*(a suffix used for days of the months)*	L 6
Nichi-yōbi	日曜日	*Sunday*	L 7
Ni-gatsu	二月	*February*	L 8
Nihon	日本	*Japan*	L 2
Nihon-go	日本語	*Japanese language*	L 16
Nihon-jin	日本人	*Japanese (person)*	L 2
ni-jū	二十	*20*	L 4
nimotsu	荷物	*luggage*	L 21
-nin	人	*(a suffix used for persons)*	L 11
ningyō	人形	*doll*	L 14
Nippon	日本	*Japan*	L 2
Nippon-go	日本語	*Japanese language*	L 16
Nippon-jin	日本人	*Japanese (person)*	L 2
no	の	*of; for*	L 1
~ no hidari	〜の左	*on/to the left of ~*	L 3
~ no mae	〜の前	*in front of ~*	L 3
~ no migi	〜の右	*on/to the right of ~*	L 3
~ no naka	〜の中	*in/inside ~*	L 10
~ no ue	〜の上	*on top of ~*	L 10
~ no ushiro	〜の後ろ	*at the back of/behind ~*	L 3
nomu	飲む	*to drink*	L 13
nugu	脱ぐ	*to take off (a coat)*	L 21
o	を	*(an object marker)*	L 13
o-	お	*(an honorific prefix)*	L 1
o-cha	お茶	*green tea*	L 13
ōfuku	往復	*round-trip*	L 19
O-genki desu ka?	お元気ですか。	*How are you?/Are you well?*	L 1
Ohayō gozaimasu.	おはようございます。	*Good morning.*	L 1
o-kane	お金	*money*	L 19
o-kā-san	お母さん	*someone else's mother; Mother! (polite)*	L 8
o-kashi	お菓子	*sweets*	L 15
ōkii	大きい	*big*	L 14
okiru	起きる	*to get up/arise*	L 13
oku	置く	*to put/leave (a luggage)*	L 21
o-miyage	お土産	*souvenir*	L 13

omocha	おもちゃ	*toy*	L 14
o-negai	お願い	*request*	L 9
O-negai shimasu.	お願いします。	*Please. (lit., I make a request.)*	L 9
ongaku	音楽	*music*	L 17
onna	女	*female (person)*	L 11
onna no hito	女の人	*a woman*	L 11
o-nomimono	お飲物	*a drink*	L 9
onsen	温泉	*hot spring*	L 18
Ōsaka	大阪	*Osaka (a city name)*	L 5
Ōsaka-jo	大阪城	*Osaka Castle*	L 5
oshieru	教える	*to teach*	L 16
osoi	遅い	*slow*	L 18
osu	押す	*to push*	L 19
o-sushi	お寿司	*Japanese cuisine made with vinegared rice and raw fish*	L 16
Ōta	太田	(a family name)	L 10
o-tearai	お手洗い	*rest room*	L 3
o-tera	お寺	*Buddhist temple*	L 13
otoko	男	*male (person)*	L 11
otoko no hito	男の人	*a man*	L 11
o-tō-san	お父さん	*someone else's father; Father! (polite)*	L 8
ototoi	おととい	*the day before yesterday*	L 15
O-yasumi-nasai.	おやすみなさい。	*Good night.*	L 1
oyogu	泳ぐ	*to swim*	L 16
pan-ya	パン屋	*bakery*	L 3
pātii	パーティー	*party*	L 20
rai-getsu	来月	*next month*	L 8
rai-shū	来週	*next week*	L 7
raku	楽	*comfortable*	L 18
rekishi	歴史	*history*	L 15
resutoran	レストラン	*restaurant*	L 9
ringo	リンゴ	*apple*	L 10
roku	六	*6*	L 4
Roku-gatsu	六月	*June*	L 8
roku-jū	六十	*60*	L 4
ryokan	旅館	*Japanese inn*	L 18
ryokō	旅行	*trip*	L 8
ryokō-dairiten	旅行代理店	*travel agency*	L 9
ryokō suru	旅行する	*to travel*	L 20
ryōri	料理	*cooking*	L 16
sake	酒	*Japanese rice wine*	L 9

sakka	作家	*writer*	L 1
samui	寒い	*cold*	L 8
san	三	*3*	L 4
-san	さん	(an honorific suffix added to another person's name)	L 1
San-gatsu	三月	*March*	L 8
san-jū	三十	*30*	L 4
sanpo	散歩	*walk; stroll*	L 15
sashimi	刺身	*sliced raw fish*	L 9
Satō	佐藤	(a family name)	L 1
-satsu	冊	(a counter used for bound objects)	A 3
Sayōnara/ Sayonara	さようなら／ さよなら。	*Goodbye.*	L 1
seki	席	*seat*	L 21
sen	千	*1,000*	L 14
-sen	線	(a suffix used for tracks)	L 4
sen-getsu	先月	*last month*	L 8
sensei	先生	*teacher*	L 1
sen-shū	先週	*last week*	L 7
sētā	セーター	*sweater*	L 18
shashin	写真	*photo*	L 9
shi	四	*4*	L 4
shibaraku	しばらく	*for a while; for a long time*	L 20
shichi	七	*7*	L 4
Shichi-gatsu	七月	*July*	L 8
shichi-jū	七十	*seventy*	L 4
Shi-gatsu	四月	*April*	L 8
shiki	式	*ceremony*	L 6
Shinkansen	新幹線	*the Shinkansen (the "bullet train")*	L 4
shinu	死ぬ	*to die*	L 19
shiroi	白い	*white*	L 14
Shitsurei shimasu/ shimashita.	失礼します／ しました。	*Excuse me for being/ having been impolite.*	L 1
shizuka	静か	*quiet*	L 18
shokuji	食事	*meal; dinner*	L 15
shōtai	招待	*invitation*	L 20
shōtai suru	招待する	*to invite*	L 20
-shū	週	*week*	L 7
shū-matsu	週末	*weekend*	L 18
sōbetsu-kai	送別会	*farewell party*	L 7
sō desu	そうです	*it's so; that's right*	L 3
-soku	足	(a counter used for footwear)	A 3
sore-kara	それから	*after that; then*	L 13
soshite	そして	*and; and then; also*	L 18

sotsugyō-shiki	卒業式	*graduation*	L 6
sotsugyō suru	卒業する	*to graduate*	L 20
subarashii	すばらしい	*wonderful*	L 20
Sui-yōbi	水曜日	*Wednesday*	L 7
suki	好き	*like*	L 17
sukiyaki	すきやき	*a popular Japanese dish*	L 16
Sumimasen.	すみません。	*Excuse me.*	L 3
supōtsu	スポーツ	*sport*	L 9
suru	する	*to do*	L 13
suwaru	座る	*to sit*	L 21
suu	吸う	*to smoke*	L 21
suzushii	涼しい	*cool*	L 8
tabako	タバコ	*cigarette*	L 21
taberu	食べる	*to eat*	L 13
-tai	たい	*(a suffix meaning "want to")*	L 18
taishi-kan	大使館	*embassy*	L 2
takai	高い	*expensive*	L 14
takusan	たくさん	*many (people/things)*	L 11
takushii de	タクシーで	*by taxi*	L 5
takushii-noriba	タクシー乗り場	*taxi stand*	L 3
Tanaka	田中	*(a family name)*	L 6
tanjō-bi	誕生日	*birthday*	L 6
tatemono	建物	*building*	L 2
tatsu	立つ	*to stand*	L 19
tēburu	テーブル	*table*	L 10
tegami	手紙	*letter*	L 17
Teikoku Hoteru	帝国ホテル	*the Imperial Hotel*	L 2
tenisu	テニス	*tennis*	L 16
tenki	天気	*weather*	L 8
tenpura	天ぷら	*Japanese deep-fried food*	L 9
tenran-kai	展覧会	*exhibition*	L 7
terebi	テレビ	*television*	L 20
to	と	*and*	L 17
tō	十	*ten*	L 10
Toda-san	戸田さん	*Mr./Mrs./Miss Toda*	L 1
tōi	遠い	*far*	L 5
to issho	と一緒	*together with*	L 8
tōka	十日	*the 10th*	L 6
Tōkyō	東京	*Tokyo (capital of Japan)*	L 2
Tōkyō Eki	東京駅	*Tokyo Station*	L 2
tomaru	泊まる	*to stay (at a hotel)*	L 13
tomeru	止める	*to stop (a car)*	L 21
tomodachi	友達	*friend*	L 8
tori	鳥	*bird*	L 17
toru	撮る	*to take (a picture)*	L 15

tosho-kan	図書館	*library*	L 5
tsugi	次	*next*	L 4
tsugi no densha	次の電車	*next train*	L 4
tsuitachi	一日	*the 1st*	L 6
tsukau	使う	*to use*	L 21
tsukeru	点ける	*to turn on (the light)*	L 20
tsuku	着く	*to arrive*	L 21
tsukue	机	*desk*	L 10
tsukuru	作る	*to make*	L 16
uchi	家	*house; home*	L 19
umi	海	*sea*	L 17
unchin-hyō	運賃表	*fare table*	L 19
ushiro	後ろ	*back*	L 3
uta	歌	*song*	L 16
utau	歌う	*to sing*	L 16
uwagi	上着	*jacket; coat*	L 21
wa	は	(a topic marker)	L 1
Wada	和田	(a family name)	L 20
wain	ワイン	*wine*	L 9
wakai	若い	*young*	L 11
warui	悪い	*bad*	L 8
watashi	私	*I*	L 2
-ya	屋	(a suffix used for stores)	L 3
yama	山	*mountain*	L 17
yama-nobori	山のぼり	*mountain climbing*	L 17
Yamada-san	山田さん	*Mr./Mrs./Miss Yamada*	L 6
Yasuda	安田	(a family name)	L 18
yasui	安い	*inexpensive*	L 14
yasumi	休み	*holiday; non-working day*	L 7
yasumu	休む	*to rest*	L 20
yattsu	八つ	*eight*	L 10
~yo	よ	(a particle used for emphasis meaning "I assure you.")	L 4
-yōbi	曜日	(a suffix for days of the week)	L 7
yobu	呼ぶ	*to call*	L 19
yōka	八日	*the 8th*	L 6
yokka	四日	*the 4th*	L 6
yomu	読む	*to read*	L 13
yon	四	*4*	L 4
yon-jū	四十	*40*	L 4
yottsu	四つ	*four*	L 10
yūbe	ゆうべ	*last night*	L 15

yūbin-kyoku	郵便局	*post office*	L 3
zannen	残念	*regrettable; too bad*	L 20
zasshi	雑誌	*magazine*	L 9

English–Japanese

about ~ (an approximate point in time)	**~ goro**	〜頃	L 20
about ~ (an approximate quantity)	**~ gurai**	〜ぐらい	L 5
after that; then	**sore-kara**	それから	L 13
again	**mata**	また	L 20
airplane	**hikō-ki**	飛行機	L 5
airport	**kūkō**	空港	L 2
all	**minna**	みんな	L 11
alone	**hitori**	一人	L 8
also; too	**mo**	も	L 15
A.M. *(morning)*	**gozen**	午前	L 4
America	**Amerika**	アメリカ	L 1
American (person)	**Amerika-jin**	アメリカ人	L 2
and	**to**	と	L 17
and; and then; also	**soshite**	そして	L 18
animal	**dōbutsu**	動物	L 17
apple	**ringo**	リンゴ	L 10
April	**Shi-gatsu**	四月	L 8
arrive (to)	**tsuku**	着く	L 21
arrive at (to)	**ni tsuku**	に着く	L 21
art museum	**bijutsu-kan**	美術館	L 13
Asahi Newspaper	**Asahi Shinbun**	朝日新聞	L 1
ashtray	**haizara**	灰皿	L 10
at; in (place)	**de**	で	L 13
at; in; on (place)	**ni**	に	L 9
at; on (time)	**ni**	に	L 13
at the back of/behind ~	**~ no ushiro**	〜の後ろ	L 3
Atami (famous hot spring resort)	**Atami**	熱海	L 18
August	**Hachi-gatsu**	八月	L 8
autumn	**aki**	秋	L 17
back	**ushiro**	後ろ	L 3
bad	**warui**	悪い	L 8
bakery	**pan-ya**	パン屋	L 3

bank	**ginkō**	銀行	L 2
basement	**chika**	地下	L 9
beer	**biiru**	ビール	L 9
big	**ōkii**	大きい	L 14
bird	**tori**	鳥	L 17
birthday	**tanjō-bi**	誕生日	L 6
black	**kuroi**	黒い	L 14
black tea	**kō-cha**	紅茶	L 13
blue	**aoi**	青い	L 14
blue one	**aoi-no**	青いの	L 14
book	**hon**	本	L 3
bookstore	**hon-ya**	本屋	L 3
box	**hako**	箱	L 10
breakfast	**asa-gohan**	朝ご飯	L 13
brown	**chairo**	茶色	L 14
Buddhist temple	**o-tera**	お寺	L 13
building	**tatemono**	建物	L 2
bullet train	**Shinkansen**	新幹線	L 4
bus	**basu**	バス	L 5
busy	**isogashii**	忙しい	L 20
but	**demo**	でも	L 16
button	**botan**	ボタン	L 19
buy (to)	**kau**	買う	L 13
by means of; in; with	**de**	で	L 5
by taxi	**takushii de**	タクシーで	L 5
call (to)	**yobu**	呼ぶ	L 19
camera shop	**kamera-ya**	カメラ屋	L 9
can; is able to; is possible	**dekiru**	で来る	L 16
car	**kuruma**	車	L 15
Carter-san	**Kātā-san**	カーターさん	L 1
ceremony	**shiki**	式	L 6
Certainly, sir/ma'am.	**Kashikomari-mashita.**	かしこまりました。	L 9
chair	**isu**	椅子	L 10
chopsticks	**hashi**	箸	L 21
cigarette	**tabako**	タバコ	L 21
coffee	**kōhii**	コーヒー	L 13
coffee shop	**kissaten**	喫茶店	L 9
cold	**samui**	寒い	L 8
collect	**atsumeru**	集める	L 17
college; university	**daigaku**	大学	L 19
come (to)	**kuru**	来る	L 16
comfortable	**raku**	楽	L 18
company	**kaisha**	会社	L 5
company employee	**kaisha-in**	会社員	L 1

concert	**konsāto**	コンサート	L 5
conference	**kaigi**	会議	L 5
conference room	**kaigi-shitsu**	会議室	L 10
convenient	**benri**	便利	L 18
cooking	**ryōri**	料理	L 16
cool	**suzushii**	涼しい	L 8
counter—suffixes used for:			
bound objects	**-satsu**	冊	A 3
currency	**-en**	円	L 14
days of the months	**-nichi**	日	L 6
flat objects	**-mai**	枚	A 3
floors	**-kai**	階	L 9
footwear	**-soku**	足	A 3
hours	**-jikan**	時間	L 5
long objects	**-hon**	本	A 3
minutes	**-fun**	分	L 4
ordinal numbers	**-ban**	番	L 4
persons	**-nin**	人	L 11
cup; glass	**koppu**	コップ	L 10
day before yesterday	**ototoi**	おととい	L 15
December	**Jū-ni-gatsu**	十二月	L 8
department store	**depāto**	デパート	L 5
desk	**tsukue**	机	L 10
dictionary	**jisho**	辞書	L 19
die (to)	**shinu**	死ぬ	L 19
do (to)	**suru**	する	L 13
doctor	**isha**	医者	L 1
doll	**ningyō**	人形	L 14
drink (to)	**nomu**	飲む	L 13
drink (a)	**o-nomimono**	お飲物	L 9
eat (to)	**taberu**	食べる	L 13
economics	**keizai**	経済	L 15
eight	**hachi**	八	L 4
eight (counter)	**yattsu**	八つ	L 10
eighth (the)	**yō-ka**	八日	L 6
eighty	**hachi-jū**	八十	L 4
embassy	**taishi-kan**	大使館	L 2
end of ~ (the)	**-matsu**	末	L 18
England	**Igirisu**	イギリス	L 2
English language	**Ei-go**	英語	L 16
English (person)	**Igirisu-jin**	イギリス人	L 2
enter (to)	**hairu**	入る	L 19
enter (to) [a room]	**ni hairu**	に入る	L 19
evening; night	**ban**	晩	L 13
Excuse me.	**Sumimasen.**	すみません。	L 3

Excuse me for being/ having been impolite.	**Shitsurei shimasu/ shimashita.**	失礼します／ しました。	L 1
exhibition	**tenran-kai**	展覧会	L 7
exist; there is/are (to) (for animate objects)	**iru**	いる	L 11
exist; there is/are (to) (for inanimate objects)	**aru**	ある	L 9
exist; there is/are (to) (polite for **aru**)	**gozaimasu**	ございます	L 9
expensive	**takai**	高い	L 14
far	**toi**	遠い	L 5
fare table	**unchin-hyō**	運賃表	L 19
farewell party	**sōbetsu-kai**	送別会	L 7
fast	**hayai**	速い	L 18
father (my father)	**chichi**	父	L 8
father (someone else's father; Father!)	**o-tō-san**	お父さん	L 8
February	**Ni-gatsu**	二月	L 8
female (person)	**onna**	女	L 11
fifth (the)	**itsuka**	五日	L 6
fifty	**go-jū**	五十	L 4
first (the)	**tsuitachi**	一日	L 6
first; to begin with	**mazu**	まず	L 19
five	**go**	五	L 4
five (counter)	**itsutsu**	五つ	L 10
flower shop	**hana-ya**	花屋	L 3
for a while; for a long time	**shibaraku**	しばらく	L 20
for (the purpose of)	**ni**	に	L 15
forty	**yon-jū**	四十	L 4
four	**shi/yon**	四	L 4
four (counter)	**yottsu**	四つ	L 10
fourth (the)	**yokka**	四日	L 6
France	**Furansu**	フランス	L 2
free (not busy)	**hima**	暇	L 20
French (person)	**Furansu-jin**	フランス人	L 2
French language	**Furansu-go**	フランス語	L 16
Friday	**Kin-yōbi**	金曜日	L 7
friend	**tomodachi**	友達	L 8
from	**kara**	から	L 5
from ~ to/till ~	**~ kara ~ made**	〜から〜まで	L 5
front	**mae**	前	L 3
fruit	**kudamono**	果物	L 15
Fukuda (a family name)	**Fukuda**	福田	L 16
German language	**Doitsu-go**	ドイツ語	L 16

German (person)	**Doitsu-jin**	ドイツ人	L 2
Germany	**Doitsu**	ドイツ	L 2
get up (to)	**okiru**	起きる	L 13
give (to)	**ageru**	あげる	L 20
Glad to meet you.	**Dōzo yoroshiku.**	どうぞよろしく。	L 1
go (to)	**iku**	行く	L 13
golf	**gorufu**	ゴルフ	L 16
good	**ii**	いい	L 8
good; skillful	**jōzu**	上手	L 16
Goodbye.	**Sayōnara/ Sayonara.**	さようなら／ さよなら。	L 1
Good day/afternoon.	**Konnichiwa.**	こんにちは。	L 1
Good evening.	**Konbanwa.**	こんばんは。	L 1
Good morning.	**Ohayō gozaimasu.**	おはようございます。	L 1
Good night.	**O-yasumi-nasai.**	おやすみなさい。	L 1
graduate (to)	**sotsugyō suru**	卒業する	L 20
graduation	**sotsugyō shiki**	卒業式	L 6
green tea	**o-cha**	お茶	L 13
half (past)	**-han**	半	L 4
hat; cap	**bōshi**	帽子	L 18
healthy; fine	**genki**	元気	L 1
Hello. (on the telephone)	**Moshi-moshi.**	もしもし	L 20
here	**koko**	ここ	L 3
Hikari (name of a super express Shinkansen)	**Hikari**	ひかり	L 4
history	**rekishi**	歴史	L15
holiday; non-working day	**yasumi**	休み	L 7
honorific prefix	**o-**	お	L 1
hospital	**byōin**	病院	L 3
hot	**atsui**	熱い／暑い	L 8
hot spring	**onsen**	温泉	L 18
hotel	**hoteru**	ホテル	L 2
house; home	**uchi**	家	L 19
how	**dō**	どう	L 18
how (about)	**ikaga**	いかが	L 14
How are you?/ Are you well?	**O-genki desu ka?**	お元気ですか。	L 1
How do you do?	**Hajimemashite.**	はじめまして。	L 1
how many hours	**nan-jikan**	何時間	L 5
how many (long objects)	**nan-bon**	何本	A 3
how many minutes	**nan-pun**	何分	L 5
how many (pairs)	**nan-zoku**	何足	A 3
how many persons	**nan-nin**	何人	L 11
how many (sheets)	**nan-mai**	何枚	A 3
how many things	**ikutsu**	いくつ	L 10

how many (volumes)	**nan-satsu**	何冊	A 3
how much	**ikura**	いくら	L 14
hurry (to)	**isogu**	急ぐ	L 19
I	**watashi**	私	L 2
I will receive/have.	**Itadakimasu.**	いただきます。	L 1
Imperial Hotel (the)	**Teikōku Hoteru**	帝国ホテル	L 2
in/inside ~	**~ no naka ni**	～の中に	L 10
in English	**Ei-go de**	英語で	L 19
in front of ~	**~ no mae**	～の前	L 3
inexpensive	**yasui**	安い	L 14
inn (Japanese)	**ryokan**	旅館	L 18
invitation	**shōtai**	招待	L 20
invite (to)	**shōtai suru**	招待する	L 20
is/am/are	**desu**	です	L 1
is/am/are not	**dewa arimasen**	ではありません	L 7
~ isn't it?	**~ ne.**	ね。	L 4
it's so; that's right	**sō desu**	そうです。	L 3
It was delicious.	**Gochiso-sama deshita.**	ごちそうさま でした。	L 1
jacket; coat	**uwagi**	上着	L 21
January	**Ichi-gatsu**	一月	L 8
Japan	**Ninon/Nippon**	日本	L 2
Japanese language	**Nihon-go/Nippon-go**	日本語	L 16
Japanese (person)	**Nihon-jin/Nippon-jin**	日本人	L 2
July	**Shichi-gatsu**	七月	L 8
June	**Roku-gatsu**	六月	L 8
Kabuki (traditional Japanese drama)	**Kabuki**	歌舞伎	L 2
Kabuki Theater (the)	**Kabuki-za**	歌舞伎座	L 2
Kato (a family name)	**Katō**	加藤	L 8
Kimura (a family name)	**Kimura**	木村	L 7
Kodama (name of a Shinkansen)	**Kodama**	こだま	L 5
large statue of Buddha	**daibutsu**	大仏	L 15
last month	**sen-getsu**	先月	L 8
last night	**yūbe**	ゆうべ	L 15
last week	**sen-shū**	先週	L 7
last year	**kyo-nen**	去年	L 15
left	**hidari**	左	L 3
letter	**tegami**	手紙	L 17
library	**tosho-kan**	図書館	L 5
light	**dentō**	電灯	L 20

like	**suki**	好き	L 17
little	**chotto**	ちょっと	L 14
luggage	**nimotsu**	荷物	L 21
lunch	**hiru-gohan**	昼ご飯	L 13
magazine	**zasshi**	雑誌	L 9
make (to)	**tsukuru**	作る	L 16
male (person)	**otoko**	男	L 11
man (a)	**otoko no hito**	男の人	L 11
many (people/things)	**takusan**	たくさん	L 11
March	**San-gatsu**	三月	L 8
marry (to)	**kekkon suru**	結婚する	L 20
match	**matchi**	マッチ	L 10
May	**Go-gatsu**	五月	L 8
meal; cooked rice	**gohan**	ご飯	L 13
meal; dinner	**shokuji**	食事	L 15
meet (to)	**au**	会う	L 20
Monday	**Getsu-yōbi**	月曜日	L 7
money	**o-kane**	お金	L 19
month	**-getsu**	月	L 8
more	**motto**	もっと	L 14
morning	**asa**	朝	L 13
mother (my)	**haha**	母	L 8
mother (someone else's); mother	**o-kā-san**	お母さん	L 8
mountain	**yama**	山	L 17
mountain climbing	**yama-nobori**	山のぼり	L 17
movie theater	**eiga-kan**	映画館	L 3
Mr./Mrs./Miss Hill	**Hiru-san**	ヒルさん	L 20
Mr./Mrs./Miss Toda	**Toda-san**	戸田さん	L 1
Mr./Mrs./Miss Yamada	**Yamada-san**	山田さん	L 6
Murata (a family name)	**Murata**	村田	L 15
music	**ongaku**	音楽	L 17
Nakano (a family name)	**Nakano**	中野	L 17
Nara (a city name)	**Nara**	奈良	L 15
near	**chikai**	近い	L 5
next	**tsugi**	次	L 4
next month	**rai-getsu**	来月	L 8
next train	**tsugi no densha**	次の電車	L 4
next week	**rai-shū**	来週	L 7
nine	**ku; kyū**	九	L 4
nine (counter)	**kokonotsu**	九つ	L 10
ninth (the)	**kokonoka**	九日	L 6
ninety	**kyū-jū**	九十	L 4
no	**iie**	いいえ	L 2
nonsmoking car	**kin'ensha**	禁煙車	L 21

noon; daytime	**hiru**	昼	L 13
November	**Jū-ichi-gatsu**	十一月	L 8
now	**ima**	今	L 4
nurse	**kangoshi**	看護師	L 1
October	**Jū-gatsu**	十月	L 8
of	**no**	の	L 1
oh	**ā**	ああ	L 3
Oh, I see./Is that so?	**Ā, sō desu ka?**	ああ、そうですか。	L 3
on/to the left of ~	**~ no hidari**	〜の左	L 3
on/to the right of ~	**~ no migi**	〜の右	L 3
on top of ~	**~ no ue ni**	〜の上に	L 10
once more	**mō ichido**	もう一度	L 19
one	**ichi**	一	L 4
one (counter)	**hitotsu**	一つ	L 10
one hundred	**hyaku**	百	L 14
one person	**hitori**	一人	L 11
one thousand	**sen**	千	L 14
one way	**katamichi**	片道	L 19
open (to)	**akeru**	開ける	L 20
Osaka (a city name)	**Ōsaka**	大阪	L 5
Osaka Castle	**Ōsaka-jō**	大阪城	L 5
o-sushi (Japanese cuisine made with vinegared rice and raw fish)	**o-sushi**	お寿司	L 16
Ota (a family name)	**Ōta**	太田	L 10
over there	**asoko**	あそこ	L 3
painting	**e**	絵	L 14
paper	**kami**	紙	A 3
park	**kōen**	公園	L 15
particles used for:			
emphasis (sentence-final)	**~ yo**	〜よ	L 4
an object marker	**o**	を	L13
a question marker	**ka**	か	L 1
a subject marker	**ga**	が	L 9
a topic marker	**wa**	は	L 1
party	**pātii**	パーティー	L 20
pencil	**enpitsu**	鉛筆	A 3
person	**hito**	人	L 1
person (polite)	**kata**	方	L 2
person of America (polite)	**Amerika no kata**	アメリカの方	L 2
photo	**shashin**	写真	L 9
play [the piano] (to)	**hiku**	弾く	L 18

please	**dōzo**	どうぞ	L 1
please; please give me	**kudasai**	下さい	L 14
Please. (lit., I make a request.)	**O-negai shimasu.**	お願いします。	L 9
please show	**misete kudasai**	見せて下さい。	L 14
P.M. (afternoon)	**gogo**	午後	L 4
poor; unskillful	**heta**	へた	L 16
post office	**yūbin-kyoku**	郵便局	L 3
pretty	**kirei**	きれい	L 18
push (to)	**osu**	押す	L 19
put/leave [a luggage] (to)	**oku**	置く	L 21
put in (to)	**ireru**	入れる	L 19
quiet	**shizuka**	静か	L 18
read (to)	**yomu**	読む	L 13
red	**akai**	赤い	L 14
regrettable	**zannen**	残念	L 20
reporter	**kisha**	記者	L 1
request	**o-negai**	お願い	L 9
rest (to)	**yasumu**	休む	L 20
restaurant	**resutoran**	レストラン	L 9
restroom	**o-tearai**	お手洗い	L 3
return (to)	**kaeru**	帰る	L 13
right	**migi**	右	L 3
road; street	**michi**	道	L 19
room	**heya**	部屋	L 10
round-trip	**ōfuku**	往復	L 19
saké (Japanese rice wine)	**sake**	酒	L 9
sales department	**eigyō-bu**	営業部	L 11
sashimi (sliced raw fish)	**sashimi**	刺身	L 9
Sato (a family name)	**Satō**	佐藤	L 1
Saturday	**Do-yōbi**	土曜日	L 7
say (to)	**iu**	言う	L 19
school	**gakkō**	学校	L 3
sea	**umi**	海	L 17
seat	**seki**	席	L 21
second (the)	**futsuka**	二つ	L 6
secretary	**hisho**	秘書	L 11
see; watch; look (to)	**miru**	見る	L 13
See you later/again.	**Jā, mata.**	じゃあ、また。	L 20
September	**Ku-gatsu**	九月	L 8
seven	**shichi; nana**	七	L 4
seven (counter)	**nanatsu**	七つ	L 10

seventh (the)	**nanoka**	七日	L 6
seventy	**nana-jū; shichi-jū**	七十	L 4
Shinkansen (the) (the "Bullet Train")	**Shinkansen**	新幹線	L 4
Shinto shrine	**jinja**	神社	L 15
ship	**fune**	船	L 5
shoes	**kutsu**	靴	L 18
shopping	**kaimono**	買い物	L 7
show (to)	**miseru**	見せる	L 14
shrimp	**ebi**	エビ	L 9
side (used for comparison)	**hō**	方	L 18
sightseeing	**kenbutsu**	見物	L 15
sing (to)	**utau**	歌う	L 16
sit (to)	**kakeru/suwaru**	掛ける/座る	L 21
six	**roku**	六	L 4
six (counter)	**muttsu**	六つ	L 10
sixth (the)	**muika**	六日	L 6
sixty	**roku-jū**	六十	L 4
sleep; go to bed (to)	**neru**	寝る	L 13
sliced raw tuna	**maguro no sashimi**	マグロの刺身	L 9
slow	**osoi**	遅い	L 18
slower	**motto yukkuri**	もっとゆっくり	L 19
small one	**chiisai-no**	小さいの	L 14
smaller one	**motto chiisai-no**	もっと小さいの	L 14
smoke (to)	**suu**	吸う	L 21
song	**uta**	歌	L 16
souvenir	**o-miyage**	お土産	L 13
speak (to)	**hanasu**	話す	L 16
sport	**supōtsu**	スポーツ	L 9
spring	**haru**	春	L 17
stamp	**kitte**	切手	L 17
stand (to)	**tatsu**	立つ	L 19
station	**eki**	駅	L 2
stay [at a hotel] (to)	**tomaru**	泊まる	L 13
stop [a car] (to)	**tomeru**	止める	L 21
store; shop	**mise**	店	L 19
subway	**chika-tetsu**	地下鉄	L 5
suffixes used for:			
days (special)	**-bi**	日	L 6
days of the week	**-yōbi**	曜日	L 7
honorific (added to another person's name)	**-san**	さん	L 1
language	**-go**	語	L 16
machines	**-ki**	機	L 19
months (name of)	**-gatsu**	月	L 8
nationality	**-jin**	人	L 2

o'clock/hours	**-ji**	時	L 4
stores	**-ya**	屋	L 3
tracks	**-sen**	線	L 4
"want to"	**-tai**	たい	L 18
year	**-nen**	年	L 15
sukiyaki (popular Japanese dish)	**sukiyaki**	すきやき	L 16
summer	**natsu**	夏	L 17
Sunday	**Nichi-yobi**	日曜日	L 7
supper	**ban-gohan**	晩ご飯	L 13
sweater	**sētā**	セーター	L 18
sweets	**o-kashi**	お菓子	L 15
swim (to)	**oyogu**	泳ぐ	L 16
table	**tēburu**	テーブル	L 10
table; schedule	**hyō**	表	L 19
take (a picture) (to)	**toru**	撮る	L 15
take off [a coat] (to)	**nugu**	脱ぐ	L 21
Tanaka (a family name)	**Tanaka**	田中	L 6
teach (to)	**oshieru**	教える	L 16
teacher	**sensei**	先生	L 1
telephone	**denwa**	電話	L 3
television	**terebi**	テレビ	L 20
ten	**jū**	十	L 4
ten (counter)	**tō**	十	L 10
tennis	**tenisu**	テニス	L 16
tenpura (Japanese deep-fried food)	**tenpura**	天ぷら	L 9
tenth (the)	**tōka**	十日	L 6
ten thousand	**ichi-man**	一万	L 14
terrible	**hidoi**	ひどい	L 20
Thank you.	**Arigatō.**	ありがとう。	L 3
Thank you.	**Dōmo arigatō.**	どうもありがとう。	L 4
that	**ano**	あの	L 1
that (one)	**are**	あれ	L 2
that person	**ano hito**	あの人	L 1
third (the)	**mikka**	三日	L 6
thirty	**san-jū**	三十	L 4
this	**kono**	この	L 2
this month	**kon-getsu**	今月	L 8
this morning	**kesa**	今朝	L 15
this (one)	**kore**	これ	L 2
this person/thing	**kochira**	こちら	L 1
this week	**kon-shū**	今週	L 7
three	**san**	三	L 4
three (counter)	**mittsu**	三つ	L 10
Thursday	**Moku-yōbi**	木曜日	L 7

ticket	**kippu**	切符	L 19
to (place)	**made**	まで	L 2
to (place)	**e**	へ	L 13
to (an indirect object marker)	**ni**	に	L 17
today	**kyō**	今日	L 6
together with	**to issho**	と一緒	L 8
Tokyo (capital of Japan)	**Tōkyō**	東京	L 2
Tokyo Station	**Tōkyō Eki**	東京駅	L 2
tomorrow	**ashita**	あした	L 6
tonight; this evening	**kon-ban**	今晩	L 20
toy	**omocha**	おもちゃ	L 14
train	**densha**	電車	L 4
(train) for Hakata	**Hakata-yuki**	博多行き	L 4
travel (to)	**ryokō suru**	旅行する	L 20
travel agency	**ryokō-dairiten**	旅行代理店	L 9
trip	**ryokō**	旅行	L 8
Tuesday	**Ka-yōbi**	火曜日	L 7
tuna	**maguro**	マグロ	L 9
turn off [the light] (to)	**kesu**	消す	L 20
turn on [the light] (to)	**tsukeru**	点ける	L 20
twenty	**ni-jū**	二十	L 4
two	**ni**	二	L 4
two (counter)	**futatsu**	二つ	L 10
two persons	**futari**	二人	L 11
use (to)	**tsukau**	使う	L 21
vase	**kabin**	花びん	L 14
vending machine	**jidō-hanbai-ki**	自動販売機	L 19
Wada (a family name)	**Wada**	和田	L 20
wait (to)	**matsu**	待つ	L 19
waiting-room	**machiai-shitsu**	待合室	L 21
walk; stroll	**sanpo**	散歩	L 15
warm	**atatakai**	暖かい	L 8
was; were	**deshita**	でした	L 6
was/were not	**dewa arimasen deshita**	ではありません でした	L 7
wear [a hat] (to)	**kaburu**	かぶる	L 18
wear [shoes] (to)	**haku**	履く	L 18
wear [a sweater] (to)	**kiru**	着る	L 18
weather	**tenki**	天気	L 8
wedding	**kekkon-shiki**	結婚式	L 6
Wednesday	**Sui-yōbi**	水曜日	L 7
week	**-shu**	週	L 7
weekend	**shū-matsu**	週末	L 18

Welcome.	**Irasshaimase.**	いらっしゃいませ。	L 14
what	**nan(i)**	何	L 2
what day (of the month)	**nan-nichi**	何日	L 6
what day of the week	**nan-yōbi**	何曜日	L 7
what kind of	**nan no**	何の	L 9
what time	**nan-ji**	何時	L 4
what track	**nan-ban-sen**	何番線	L 4
when	**itsu**	いつ	L 8
where	**doko**	どこ	L 2
which	**dono**	どの	L 19
which (one)	**dore**	どれ	L 19
white	**shiroi**	白い	L 14
who	**dare**	誰	L 1
window	**mado**	窓	L 20
wine	**wain**	ワイン	L 9
winter	**fuyu**	冬	L 17
woman (a)	**onna no hito**	女の人	L 11
wonderful	**subarashii**	すばらしい	L 20
write (to)	**kaku**	書く	L 17
writer	**sakka**	作家	L 1
Yasuda (a family name)	**Yasuda**	安田	L 18
yes	**hai**	はい	L 1
yes (informal)	**ē**	ええ	L 21
yesterday	**kinō**	きのう	L 6
you	**anata**	あなた	L 2
You are welcome.	**Dō-itashimashite.**	どういたしまして。	L 3
young	**wakai**	若い	L 11
your	**anata no**	あなたの	L 6